HOMiLY GRiTS 2 "Snack Food for the Soul"

Library of Congress Cataloging –in-Publication Data

VanHoose, Robert W, 1929
    Homily Grits 2, Snack Food for The Soul./Robert VanHoose
    112 p.cm
    Includes biographical references
    ISBN: 0-9742612-1-1
    1.   Christian meditations I. Title

               2003114152
               CIP

Published by Homily Grits Publishing Co.
All rights reserved. Printed in the United States of America

"Taste and see that the Lord is Good!"
HOMILY GRITS 2
"Snack Food for The Soul"

Homily Grits Publishing Co.
Ocala, Florida
www.homilygrits.com
RVanHoose@homilygrits.com

HOMILY GRITS 2 Menu

"Taste and See That the Lord is Good!"

These snacks are nourishing anytime!

Mornings with or without breakfast

Noon lunch break

Dinner as shared appetizer or dessert

Bedtime (please don't fall asleep while reading)

Welcome to Homily Grits 2!

"God works in a mysterious way, His wonders to perform!" When I started praying the "Prayer of Jabez" and asking God to expand my ministry opportunities, I never dreamed that it would be through writing books.

It has been a "sacred delight" for me to see how God has spoken to so many in so many different ways through these applications of His Word.

My fervent prayer for you and all who read this book is that you will be greatly blessed, encouraged, comforted, and strengthened in your faith through these devotions.

Most of all, I pray that these efforts will be pleasing in God's sight, and that He will be glorified.

Thank you for the privilege of sharing God's love with you through Homily Grits. To God alone be the glory.

In His Love,

Robert W. VanHoose

Dedicated with love to our grandchildren:

(Trey) Robert W. VanHoose III
Stephen VanHoose
Joe VanHoose
Stephanie Hudson
Stacey Hudson
Jonathan VanHoose
Kirby VanHoose
Irene Butler
Kelly Hudson
Lauren Puig
"RJ" Puig

"But the love of the LORD remains forever
with those who fear him.
His salvation extends to the children's children
of those who are faithful to his covenant,"
-Psalm 103:17,18a NLT

Can You Hear Me Now?

"And I will give you treasures hidden in the darkness – secret riches. I will do this so you may know that I am the LORD, the God of Israel, the one who calls you by name." Isaiah 45:3 NLT

If the theory of evolution were true, we would soon see babies being born with cell phones growing out of their ears. These instant communication tools are everywhere.

> *"Happy are those who hear the joyful call to worship, for they will walk in the light of your presence, Lord."*
> *Psalm 89:15 NLT*

When the TV ad features "can you hear me now?" it is echoing God's cry since the beginning of time as He has softly and tenderly and loudly and angrily called His children to repentance and relationship.

The children of Israel were world class hearing impaired rebels. God spoke to them through a burning bush, a pillar of clouds by day and a fire by night, but all his calls were soon forgotten by a bunch of spoiled brats who were hard to satisfy but easy to be lead astray by every self centered concern and distraction.

Before we become too critical of the Children of Israel, we need to ask ourselves whether we are hearing God today. He gives His call to salvation and many have to be flat on their backs looking up before they hear, and others remain deaf.

He calls all believers to the ongoing process of sanctification and many have a connection problem as to what holy living is all about.

He calls all believers to service for which He has equipped us to accomplish His purposes which He planned for us even before we were born. Why oh why don't we have more passion to hear and be faithful to this calling, whatever it might be?

> *"But even more blessed are all who hear the Word of God and put it into practice."*
> *Matthew 13:17 NLT*

God calls all believers to worship individually and corporately so that the other calls may be manifested in us and others through us. Can you hear Him now?

Father, help me to turn off my mute button so that I can hear all of your calls loud and clear. Amen

1

What the Locusts Have Taken

"In his kindness God called you to his eternal glory by means of Jesus Christ. After you have suffered a little while, he will restore, support, and strengthen you, and he will place you on a firm foundation. All power is his forever and ever." 1 Peter 5:10, 11 NLT

Whether referring to swarms of locusts symbolically or literally, this prophecy in Joel paints a frightening picture.

> *"You have rejected us, O God, and broken our defenses. You have been angry with us; now restore us to your favor."*
> *Psalm 60:1 NLT*

Whether forthtelling a real plague of locusts, or the destruction of Jerusalem, or to the fire that is going to test the wood, hay, and stubble of our lives on judgment day, the real message is repentance!

On a personal level, we can liken the locusts to all of the afflictions that plagued Job, or to the locusts of sin that sometimes consume and seek to destroy us.

Job was told to "curse God and die". David was consumed by guilt and had to endure the consequences of his sin with Bathsheba. The prodigal son was down to eating slop with the hogs before his plague ended.

When we drop our guard and the great deceiver sneaks in and overcomes us, we get so overcome by guilt and remorse that we are made to doubt our salvation and wonder whether we are really saved.

It is at these times when we get an idea of what Joel is talking about. When we bring our broken hearts to the throne of grace in true repentance; the restoration that God promises and demonstrates in the lives of Job, David, and the prodigal son will be ours.

> *"The LORD says, "I will give you back what you lost to the stripping locusts, the cutting locusts, the swarming locusts, and the hopping locusts"*
> *Joel 2:25 NIV*

Father, thank you for restoring what the locusts have eaten through the trials of my life, and for giving me assurance that I will be protected and covered by your righteousness on judgment day. Amen

Till Misery Do Us Part?

"Therefore shall a man leave his father and his mother, and shall cleave unto his wife: and they shall be one flesh." Genesis 2:24

Do you know of anyone who has gone into a marriage hoping to

> *" Blessed is everyone who fears the LORD, who walks in His ways"*
> *Psalm 128:1*

become miserable or to make life miserable for their spouse? What is it that turns the highest of expectations into depths of misery?

A Christian counselor friend of mine says that people who have found misery in marriage will find the root cause in Genesis 2:24. It is either problems with leaving, cleaving, or becoming one flesh.

Leaving family, life style, and all sorts of other accumulated baggage is often not easy. Different backgrounds are especially difficult. Like oil and water believers and non believers don't mix, and sooner or later this will lead to real misery in most cases.

Lack of real cleaving or commitment has made the idea of going into marriage in a disposable, no deposit no return bottle very popular. When we go in thinking we can go out any time we don't get our way, choose not to forgive and forget, and not to honor the commitment made, we are already planting the seeds of disaster. Children, not childishness are supposed to be the fruit of a marriage. When God is not taken into a marriage, the "tie that binds" has no knot.

Perceived lack of sexual satisfaction is often a problem. It is interesting to note that surveys find that couples who went into marriage as virgins report much more sexual satisfaction in their marriage.. This is another indication that God's way to sexual satisfaction is the best way.

> *"Nevertheless let each one of you in particular so love his own wife as himself, and let the wife see that she respects her husband."*
> *Ephesians 5:33*

Any good marriage requires a lot of unconditional love. We must learn to love unconditionally, just as God loves us, not because of our shortcomings and sins, but in spite of them.

Father help me to understand and practice the essentials of a happy marriage. Amen

3

Designer Labels

"For whoever finds Me finds life and wins approval from the LORD. But those who miss Me have injured themselves. All who hate Me love death." Proverbs 8:35 (NLT)

Teenagers seem to place great importance on wearing the right brands

> *"And may the Lord our God show us his approval and make our efforts successful. Yes, make our efforts successful!"*
> *Psalm 90:17 NLT*

as a means of acquiring self esteem. We seem to have a tendency to want to validate our worth and the approval of our peers by the clothes we wear, the cars we drive, the houses we live in and sometimes even the church we attend.

Many churches sometimes seem to be establishing their own "designer label" by their traditions of worship, interpretations of Scripture, and ideas about how the grace of God is dispensed.

Frankly, God couldn't care less about your outward appearance and your denominational or socio economic labels. He cares only about your heart, and your relationship with Him!

God is the great designer of us all. He created us in His image, for His pleasure, and for His purposes, and for eternity. In His love, He created us with a free will so that we could be free to love Him and fellowship with Him. Unfortunately, this free will led to disobedience by Adam and Eve, and sin entered the world, destroying the earthly paradise that God had created for us.

In His mercy, God ordained that paradise and fellowship with Him would be restored for now and forever by the life, death, and resurrection of His Son, and our Savior, Jesus Christ, for all who believe this, and come into a personal faith relationship with Jesus Christ.

> *"Your approval or disapproval means nothing to me, because I know you don't have God's love within you"*
> *John 5:41 NLT*

The designer label "righteous" which we will wear by faith when we stand before God is the only label that really matters. Are you wearing this label?

Father, keep me ever mindful that it's not the label on my back, but my relationship with You that counts. Amen

Read 1 Peter 4:1-11 **Numbers 11:1-24**

Don't Shrink Wrap God!

"Ah, Lord GOD! Behold, You have made the heavens and the earth by Your great power and outstretched arm. There is nothing too hard for You." Jeremiah 32:17

Shrink wrap packaging has become one of great minor irritations of my

> **"And the Lord said to Moses, "Has the Lord's arm been shortened?" Numbers 11:23**

life. Whether to prevent tampering, or shrinking by theft, everything seems to come "shrink wrapped".

I have a college degree and at least normal intelligence, but to get that sack of candy open without tearing up the whole sack, to get that slice of ham out of that "new and improved" zip lock pack, continues to frustrate me. I just wish that whoever devised some of the packaging on cd wrappers, computer software, and those postage stamp sized items wrapped in a package too big to slip in your pocket would have to share my frustration in trying to get them open.

Unfortunately, most of us have the tendency to "shrink wrap" God by boxing Him in to only a small portion of our hearts, our minds and our wills so that we miss out on so many of the blessings and joy that He would like to give us.

We shrink Him by failing to grow in our knowledge and understanding of Him through studying His Word, by trusting Him with our salvation, but not with our pocketbooks; our time on Sunday mornings but not the rest of the week.

The Great I AM, who not only ordains but deserves to be the top priority in our lives, is thwarted in His desire to accomplish His purposes for us and through us as we continue to put ourselves and our desires ahead of Him.

> **"Do it with all the strength and energy that God supplies. Then God will be given glory in everything through Jesus Christ. All glory and power belong to him forever and ever. Amen" 1 Peter 4:11 NLT**

It's time to "take off the wraps" and let God take complete control of our lives and grow into the fullness of His love and His power.

Father, give me a faith as big as Your love and in the power of Your Spirit, help me to find out what real living is all about. Amen

Taking Inventory

"Not that I seek the gift, but I seek the fruit that abounds to your account." Philippians 4:17

An accurate inventory of cash, receivables, merchandise, supplies and

> *"Moreover by them your servant is warned, and in keeping them is great reward."*
> *Psalm 19:11*

equipment is the only way any business can determine whether it made a profit or loss, detect theft or pilferage, and come up with a net worth.

On the personal level, when we add our cash, savings, investments, and possessions, and subtract what we owe, we determine our personal net worth.

On the spiritual level, we all need to be constantly taking inventory of the debit and credit balances in God's book of life. Scripture tells us that our faith in Jesus Christ has been credited as righteousness by God, with overdraft protection. Because of this imputed righteousness our destination is assured. Heaven is a gift and we do not earn it!

Scripture also tells us that when arrive at our heavenly destination there is going to be an inventory taken of all the treasures we have stored up in heaven consisting of the good works we did and fruit we produced that glorified God during our sojourn on earth. These are what will remain after the fire has burned away the "wood, hay and straw" of wasted lives and missed opportunities.

We will find our account credited for loving God and others, for bringing others to Christ, and those things through which we have t gloriied God On a personal, private, public, and church level.

> *"Store up your treasures in heaven, where they will never become moth-eaten or rusty and where they will be safe from thieves."*
> *Matthew 6:20 NLT*

To be called "good and faithful servant" by God and to be given even more ministry privileges in heaven are opportunities we surely don't want to miss.

Father, thank you for taking the cup of death for the wages of sin away from me by sending Jesus to die for my sins on the Cross at Calvary. Amen

How Do you Like your Eggs?
"Restore to me again the joy of Your salvation, and make me willing to obey You." Psalm 51:12 NLT

Nobody likes to get "egg in the face" by committing some big blunder or making a bad choice. Once the yolk is broken, and the egg whites and yolks are mixed, you surely can't have your eggs unscrambled!

> *"You have forgiven the iniquity of Your people; You have covered all their sin"*
> *Psalm 85:2*

The lives of Christians are filled with growth pills disguised as problems. God often arranges circumstances to discipline, test, humble, and confound us in the process of refining us and conforming us into the image of Christ.

Most of the time, we make the beds that we have to lie in through willful disobedience and trading God control for self control, and we have to suffer the consequences that often will plague us for the rest of our lives.

The question is not if, but when we get egg in our face, undergo God's discipline and chastening, or slip into our flesh mode, how do we respond? We can blame others, rationalize, deny, fall into self pity and feeling sorry for ourselves. The worst mistake we can make is to get angry at God.

That "roaring lion" is just waiting to step up when we step down to self centered justification instead of Christ centered confession and repentance.

When we "blow it" we join an all star lineup of Saints who did the same thing. Starting with Adam and Eve, Moses, Jonah, David, Peter and Paul, just to name a few.

> *"But may the God of all grace, who called us to His eternal glory by Christ Jesus, after you have suffered a while, perfect, establish, strengthen, and settle you."*
> *1 Peter 5:10*

When the "Master Chef" seasons our sins with forgiveness and grace, he can turn our "scrambled eggs" into an omelet fit to serve the King!

Father, help me to know that You are always more ready to forgive than I am to be forgiven. Amen

Rice Krispie Religion

"If you are filled with light, with no dark corners, then your whole life will be radiant, as though a floodlight is shining on you." Luke 11:36 NLT

Rice Krispies have been around for 3 generations or longer, and still going strong. They are even better in cookies. I have always enjoyed the rice krispie "snap, crackle, and pop" when you add milk to the cereal and it begins to explode. Gotta be careful or all those kernels will rise to the top and overflow the bowl. I have noticed they are not nearly as good if you let them sit and get squishy

> *"I will be filled with joy because of you. I will sing praises to your name, O Most High."*
> *Psalm 9:2 NLT*

There is a lot of wonderful "snap, crackle, and pop" when the pure milk of the gospel is poured into a receptive kernel. We are told that there is great rejoicing in heaven when a sinner repents and receives Jesus as Savior. .

The "snap, crackle, and pop" passion of the new birth in Christ experienced by many believers is not unlike falling in love and getting married. We enjoy a great emotional high and are filled with overflowing joy and passion. Great as the feelings are, they will not always be enough to sustain a healthy growing relationship with God or with our spouse.

The key to both is in growing into maturity. We should never let either relationship stand still and get mired down in selfishness, self centered behavior or overcome by the assaults of the flesh, the world, or the devil.

As we grow in our love relationship with Christ, the "snap,crackle, and pop" of passion can only be sustained by being nourished by His Word daily, and getting to know Him by experience as we grow into the fullness of Christ.

As we grow in our love relationship with our spouses, we need the sustaining power of the fruit of the Spirit and the nourishing power of love if we are to maintain the "snap, crackle and pop" during our life together.

> *"No wonder my heart is filled with joy,and my mouth shouts his praises!"*
> *Acts 2:26 NLT*

Father, thank you for the sacred delight that is mine through my growing and abiding relationship with You. Amen

8

Whose Shoes?

"For shoes, put on the peace that comes from the Good News, so that you will be fully prepared." Ephesians 6:15 NLT

Athletic shoes are a multi billion dollar business. Nike, Reebok, Addidas, and others pay hundreds of millions of dollars just to get athletes to wear and endorse shoes when many wouldn't want to be caught dead in some of their shoes.

> *"How beautiful on the mountains are the feet of those who bring good news of peace and salvation, the news that the God of Israel reigns!"*
> *Isaiah 52:7 NLT*

John said that he was not worthy even to carry Jesus's shoes, much less walk in them. Children of very famous and successful parents, successors of legendary coaches, athletes, and even preachers are often reminded of the "big shoes" they have to fill. Often the burden of trying to "fill the shoes" is too great, and those who try end up defeated and destroyed in the process.

Sandals were the footwear of biblical days, and apparently socks had not been invented. This caused a lot of dust and dirt to accumulate on the feet as people walked and worked in sandals, necessitating the removing of sandals and washing of feet by the lowliest of servants when anyone entered the homes of the high and mighty of those days.

No wonder the disciples were taken back when their leader and who they thought would be king and ruler of the world stooped to perform the lowliest task of the lowliest of slaves or servants when he washed their feet.

Whether barefoot or walking in $200 Nike's, we need to walk in humility with the one who filled the shoes that we could never fill. He lived a perfect life for us that we could never live for ourselves in order to fill the demands of the law for us that we could never keep for ourselves. He washed and cleansed us forever in the sight of God with His own blood. When we walk by faith in the good news, we are wearing the shoes of the real champion.

> *"If I then, your Lord and Teacher, have washed your feet, you also ought to wash one another's feet."*
> *John 13:14*

Father, keep my ever mindful to "walk the walk" of peace that comes from the "good news". Amen

9

The Ingrown Church

"You also, like living stones, are being built into a spiritual house to be a holy priesthood, offering spiritual sacrifices acceptable to God through Jesus Christ." 1 Peter 2:5 NIV

The body of Christ is a vital, living organism. If it is not growing, it is not healthy. The fact that thousands of churches are closing every year, and thousands of others are losing members and especially youth in droves begs the question "why"?

> *"My soul yearns, even faints, for the courts of the LORD;my heart and my flesh cry out for the living God."*
> *Psalm 84:2 NIV*

One of the big reasons that I have seen is that many churches and seemingly many denominations have become ingrown. Focus is too often on worshipping tradition and defending the faith rather than on obeying the great commandment and great commission.

Many ingrown churches seem to be operating more as sanctuaries for saints rather than hospitals for sinners. They "major in minors".

There are many vital, doctrinally sound, bible believing churches growing by leaps and bounds throughout the country. These contradict the rationalization of the dying churches that hide behind the excuse that their "purity of doctrine" is weeding out the unbelievers, and that numbers do not mean anything.

We are called to be "contagious Christians" in churches where God is at work through ministry within and without. Church should be a place that we can't wait to get to to celebrate the love, peace, and joy of our salvation in Christ through authentic worship that encourages us, other believers, and any seekers who might show up on any given Sunday.

> *"I know your deeds; you have a reputation of being alive, but you are dead. Wake up! Strengthen what remains and is about to die, for I have not found your deeds complete in the sight of my God."*
> *Revelation 3:1b,2 NIV*

We need to be conservative in doctrine, and liberal in love. Growing within doesn't mean being ingrown. We cannot grow within without growing out in ministry.

Father, keep me ever mindful that you are alive and relevant, and let your church be true to its calling. Amen

When is Enough not Enough?

"You say, 'I am rich; I have acquired wealth and do not need a thing.' But you do not realize that you are wretched, pitiful, poor, blind and naked. " Revelation 3: 17 NIV

Idolatry is one the greatest sources of unhappiness and dissatisfaction in the world today. When we become possessed by possessions, power, prestige, lust or any trivial pursuits, we can never know the joy and Godly contentment of having the peace that surpasses all understanding. When we worship at the throne of any of these idols, enough will never be enough – we will always want more!

> *"Blessed is the man who makes the LORD his trust, who does not look to the proud, to those who turn aside to false gods."*
> *Psalm 40:4 NIV*

Becoming driven by the need to validate our worth and seeking happiness through anything other than a right relationship with God through faith in Jesus Christ is driving down the highway to despair.

These idols will, usually sooner than later, turn out to be the false gods that they are, and we are left holding the bag of emptiness.

When we have the blessings of true joy, knowing the love of God and others, learning to be content in knowing that God's power is made perfect in our weaknesses, and that He will supply His all sufficient grace and meet our every need according to His riches in Christ Jesus, we have more than enough.

We will have more than enough love so that we can pass some on to others. We will have more than enough forgiveness so that we can pass some on others, and we will have more than enough joy go around.

Without this, we will never enjoy life to the fullest.

> *"For you have spent enough time in the past doing what pagans choose to do--living in debauchery, lust, drunkenness, orgies, carousing and detestable idolatry"*
> *1 Peter 4:3 NIV*

Father, let abiding in You through Your Word be more than enough for me. Amen

Tent Dwellers Arise!

"I think it is right to refresh your memory as long as I live in the tent of this body, because I know that I will soon put it aside, as our Lord Jesus Christ has made clear to me." 2 Peter 1:13,14 NIV

God has been a tent dweller for many generations. In Exodus 40:34 we find:*" Then the cloud covered the Tent of Meeting, and the glory of the Lord filled the tabernacle"* God's presence filled the tent of meeting, and only left the tent to dwell in the temple. When Jesus Christ died on the cross, God's presence left the temple and took up residence of these earthly tents in which we live.

> *" If you make the Most High your dwelling- even the LORD , who is my refuge - then no harm will befall you, no disaster will come near your tent."*
> *Psalm 91:9,10 NIV*

There is nothing permanent about tents. They endure the wind and rain, snow and hail, and start wearing out the day they are pitched. This tent we are living in is not permanent either. It starts dying the day we are born, and sooner or later we are going to have to leave it.

The good news for believers is that we are going to receive a brand new, incorruptible, permanent home at the resurrection of the just. Our new one will know no more suffering, no more pain, no more destruction, no more tears.

> *"Now we know that if the earthly tent we live in is destroyed, we have a building from God, an eternal house in heaven, not built by human hands"*
> *2 Corinthians 5:1 NIV*

The master builder with a master plan has even sent His son ahead to prepare a place for us and our new permanent home. It is going to be so wonderful we cannot begin to comprehend. As Paul says: "No eye has seen, no ear has heard, no mind has conceived what God has prepared for those who love Him"[1 Corinthians 2:9)

Father as I get older and more aware of how temporary my tent is. help me to "keep my eye on the prize" and be comforted by Your peace and joy. Amen

Read John 6:23-58   Psalm 78:17-39

Subway Religion

"He humbled you, causing you to hunger and then feeding you with manna, which neither you nor your fathers had known, to teach you that man does not live on bread alone but on every word that comes from the mouth of the LORD" Deuteronomy 8:3 NIV

Only Christ's church offers more franchise locations and more varieties of bread than Subway sandwich shops. Christ's church serves the "bread of life" at hundreds of Christian denominations throughout the world!

> *"They ate the food of angels! God gave them all they could hold."*
> *Psalm 78:25 NLT*

Perhaps our creator, who made us all with many different physical, mental, and emotional makeups, allowed man to bring denominations into His church so that we could all find a place to worship in the heart language that He has given us.

Some denominations serve the bread of life with "a little bit country". Others feature "a little bit rock and roll". Whether you like formal or casual, traditional or contemporary, storefronts or cathedrals, you can find a place to worship just right for you. It's not the label, but the heart that counts.

Our freedom and liberty in Christ gives us a lot of latitude as to how and where we can worship. As long as salvation by grace alone, through faith in Jesus Christ alone, by authority of the inerrant truth of Scripture alone is proclaimed, God will be present and pleased with wherever we choose to worship.

The world has been in the church for many centuries, and brought a lot of heresy and false teachings. Truth has too often become relative truth. Tradition and legalism have overtaken relationship and mission, and hypocritical glory too often robs God of His glory.

> *"Jesus replied, "I am the bread of life. No one who comes to me will ever be hungry again. Those who believe in me will never thirst."*
> *John 6:35 NLT*

Perhaps now, more than ever before, we should "beware of the leaven of the scribes and Pharisees", as we seek to worship God in spirit and in truth.

Father, fill me with all wisdom and spiritual discernment that I might feed on the true bread of life. Amen

13

Not What but Who

"I will give them a heart to know me, that I am the LORD . They will be my people, and I will be their God, for they will return to me with all their heart. Jeremiah 24:7

The Scribes and the Pharisees thought that they knew all there was to

> *"Continue your love to those who know you, your righteousness to the upright in heart."*
> *Psalm 36:10 NIV*

know about God. They spent a lifetime in study, prayer, and observing the law,and yet our Lord called them a "brood of vipers". (Matthew 3:7)

Our Lord also said: "But blessed are your eyes because they see, and your ears because they hear. "For I tell you the truth, many prophets and righteous men longed to see what you see but did not see it, and to hear what you hear but did not hear it."(Matthew 13:11).

The key to the kingdom of God and receiving the righteousness of Christ is found in John 17:3: "Now this is eternal life: that they may know you, the only true God, and Jesus Christ, whom you have sent"

Clearly, our eternal life is not based on what we know but on Who we know! God calls us into a close and personal relationship with His Son and our brother, Jesus Christ. Eternal life begins the minute we know Him by faith as our Savior. It continues as we grow into His fullness by getting to know Him as He speaks to us through His Word, through prayer, through circumstances, and through other believers.

We can and should learn to know as much about God as we can, but we need to always remember it's not what we know, but who we know that counts!

The Pharisees made religion their god, and as a result, did not have God in their religion. Many seem to acquire a lot of head knowledge and doctrinal knowledge without having a clue as to what heart knowledge is all about. Unless we have Jesus in our hearts, all of the sacraments and ordinances of any church are worthless.

> *"We know that we have come to know him if we obey his commands"*
> *1 John 2:3 NIV*

Father, keep me ever mindful that knowing You through a real and personal relationship with Your Son is what's really important. Amen

Are You Full of It?

"So now we can rejoice in our wonderful new relationship with God--all because of what our Lord Jesus Christ has done for us in making us friends of God." Romans 5:11 NLT

"Delight", "happiness", "satisfaction", "bliss", "exceptionally good": all of these words are used to define one little word – joy! Scripture after Scripture affirms that joy should be an integral part of the life of every Christian.

> *"But let all who take refuge in you rejoice; let them sing joyful praises forever. Protect them, so all who love your name may be filled with joy"*
> *Psalm 5:11 NLT*

Unfortunately we Christians all too often lose sight of the fact that Jesus said: "I have told you this so that you will be filled with my joy. Yes, your joy will overflow!" (John 15:11)

It is this joy in the Lord and what He has done for us which turns our "have to" into "want to". The joy of the Lord makes us want to do the things that please Him.

God, who loves us with an everlasting love, "loves a cheerful giver", one who gives treasures, time, and talents out of joy and not out of compulsion.

We sing: "the joy of the Lord is my strength", and many other hymns of joy. 1 John 1:4 says: "We are writing these things so that your joy will be complete." St Paul says in Philippians 4:4: "Always be full of joy in the Lord. I say it again--rejoice!"

When people, circumstances, or things try to rob you of your joy; always remember that the joy of the Lord is your strength and your peace. Let your joy overflow into the lives of all those around youl

> *"We can rejoice, too, when we run into problems and trials, for we know that they are good for us--they help us learn to endure."*
> *Romans 5:3 NLT*

Father, let nothing or no one rob me of my joy that I have in You. Amen

R U A POT?

"Do not judge, and you will not be judged. Do not condemn, and you will not be condemned. Forgive, and you will be forgiven." Luke 6:37 NIV

Too many of us seem to enjoy and spend too much time worrying about those "kettles". When our fleshly critical and judgmental spirits take over, grace gets cast aside and we have a ball making ourselves feel good by making others look bad.

> *"And the heavens proclaim his righteousness, for God himself is judge."*
> *Psalm 50:6 NIV*

Many seem to have a need to feel that they are better than some one else. Racial and religious prejudice and discrimination spring from this root cause. The victims of such prejudice often turn right around and practice the same thing against others they deem further down the economic, racial, or social ladder. Sadly, many pastors and many churches are the worst offenders.

While we need to recognize and hate sin of all kinds, admonish our brothers and sisters in Christ in Christian love when their sinful behavior calls for it; we must be like Christ, who always hated the sin, but always loved the sinners, except the self righteousness and hypocrisy of the Scribes and Pharisees.

Scripture teaches that we would be better off spending our time judging ourselves. "But if we judged ourselves, we would not come under judgment." (1 Corinthians 11:31 NIV)

> *"You, therefore, have no excuse, you who pass judgment on someone else, for at whatever point you judge the other, you are condemning yourself, because you who pass judgment do the same things."*
> *Romans 2:1 NIV*

Frankly, I cannot afford the luxury of judging, condemning, and not forgiving others. I need all of the grace and mercy available to atone for my own sins, and I dare not forget our Lord's warning:"But if you do not forgive men their sins, your Father will not forgive your sins." Matthew 6:15 NIV)

Father, take away my critical, judgmental spirit, and replace it with Your grace that abounds even more than sin. Amen

Have you "Defragged" Lately?

"Create in me a clean heart, O God. Renew a right spirit within me. Do not banish me from your presence, and don't take your Holy Spirit from me. Restore to me again the joy of your salvation, and make me willing to obey you." Psalm 51:10-12 NLT

While only the computer literate have ever heard of "defragging" it's not a bad concept for all believers. Simply put, it's an operation whereby all fragments on your computer's hard disk are consolidated, and disk space is freed up. This, along with disk clean up can make remarkable improvement in the operation of a computer.

> "How can I know all the sins lurking in my heart? Cleanse me from these hidden faults."
> Psalm 19:12 NLT

If we are ever going to grow into the fullness of Christ we need constant "defragging" and clean up of our minds and souls.

When we take our sins and burdens to the cross, we free up our strength and energy to be filled with the love of God and the strength of His Spirit.

When we confess and dump any lingering bitterness or resentment, we free up a lot of wasted space for joy. When we dump any jealousy, envy, lust, or idolatry, we are freed to become Christ centered instead of self centered. When we get rid of anger and impatience, we make room for that "peace that surpasses all understanding." When we get rid of all the fragments of time wasted on trivial pursuits, we free up time to be about our Father's business – doing those things for which He created us.

Thanks be to God that He has given us the means for continual "defragging" and clean up through daily confession, repentance, and abiding in the power of the Holy Spirit.

> "Therefore, cleanse your sinful hearts and stop being stubborn."
> Deuteronomy 10:16 NLT

Father, equip me to "fight the good fight" and "run the good race" by getting rid of all those things that hold me back. Amen

The Heart of the Matter

"And I will give you a new heart with new and right desires, and I will put a new spirit in you. I will take out your stony heart of sin and give you a new, obedient heart. And I will put my Spirit in you so you will obey my laws and do whatever I command. Ezekial 36:26,27 NLT

Heart disease is not only the #1 cause of physical death, it is also the #1 cause of spiritual death.

> *"God is my shield, saving those whose hearts are true and right."*
> *Psalm 7:10 NLT*

Daily miracles are now commonplace throughout the world. God has provided skilled doctors to deal with heart disease as never before. However, sooner or later hearts are going to stop beating, and all are going to die physically.

As sin and man's inhumanity to man becomes increasingly worse throughout the world we need to understand the "heart of the matter" is that only God can change hearts.

Rather than pray for world peace, an end to abortions, pain and suffering in the world, it might be better to ask God to have mercy on this sin-sick, depraved world, and bring heart changing renewal, revival, and rebirth.

When the hearts filled with hatred, jealousy, prejudice, deceit, and all of the other sins that seem to plague this world receive a transplant and become alive in Christ and filled with the love of God which is ours through faith in Christ Jesus, everything else will fall into place.

God is looking into the heart of believers and unbelievers alike, and can seldom be liking what He sees. So far, in His forebearing, longsuffering, patient, and merciful love, He has allowed sin, death and destruction to run its course and have its way.

How much longer His grace will abound over the sin of the world is cause for concern especially for the billions of people who have not received a heart transplant. This is the "heart of the matter".

> *"Realizing this man's understanding, Jesus said to him, "You are not far from the Kingdom of God."*
> *Mark 12:34 NLT*

Father, bring renewal and revival into the world, and let it begin within me. Amen

Watch out for the Minefields!

"Be self controlled and alert. Your enemy the devil prowls around like a roaring lion looking for someone to devour." 1 Peter 5:8 NIV

Minefields planted during a war seem to harm and plague the people

> *"Keep me from the snares they have laid for me, from the traps set by evildoers"*
> *Psalm 141.9 NIV*

for years after the war is over. Unsuspecting children and adults have stepped on one years later and been killed or severely injured.

Although the war is over and satan has been defeated the battlefield of life is still strewn with minefields through which he seeks to destroy our faith and control our baser instincts.

We too often forget that life is a battleground where we walk daily through the minefields planted by the sins of the world in addition to pride, idolatry, anger, lust, jealousy, and other rebellion against God.

This is the battleground through which our Savior walked without tripping on any of the mines, and defused them by His death on the cross so that they no longer have the power to destroy us.

We should also remember that although they cannot destroy us they can cause great harm to us, to those we love, and to the cause of Christ. This is why it is so important that we daily "put on the full armor of God, so that when the day of evil comes, you may be able to stand your ground, and after you have done everything, to stand."(Ephesians 6:13)

> *"Everything we do wrong is sin, but not all sin is fatal.*
> *We know that none of the God-begotten makes a practice of sin-- fatal sin. The God-begotten are also the God-protected. The Evil One can't lay a hand on them."*
> *1 John 5:17,18 MSG*

Father, by the power of Your Spirit, protect me from the minefields that are still hurtful to me and to others. Amen

Hope at the End of the Rope

"Dear brothers and sisters, whenever trouble comes your way, let it be an opportunity for joy. For when your faith is tested, your endurance has a chance to grow. So let it grow, for when your endurance is fully developed, you will be strong in character and ready for anything. James 1:2-4 NLT

Along with the cup of living water, joy, and blessings; everyone at some time or another is going to drink from the cups of sorrow and suffering.

> *"I have been dismissed as one who is dead, like a strong man with no strength left."*
> *Psalm 88:4 NLT*

Whether we grieve over the death of a loved one, a sin, a broken relationship – whether our suffering is physical, emotional, or financial, it is real and it hurts. When these hurts pile up, we sometimes find ourselves at the end of our ropes. We just can't handle anymore! The good news is that we don't have to!

We have a God who is no stranger to sorrow and suffering. "He was despised and rejected by men, a man of sorrows, and familiar with suffering. Like one from whom men hide their faces he was despised, and we esteemed him not." (Isaiah 53:3)

Our God who cannot lie is the God who works all things for our good. *"And God is faithful; he will not let you be tempted beyond what you can bear. But when you are tempted, he will also provide a way out so that you can stand up under it." (1 Corinthians 10:13)*

Rather than fall into the pit of depression and despair, we need to lay hold of the hope at the end of the rope. We need to trust in the One who loves us with an everlasting love, the One who says: *"My grace is sufficient for you, for my power is made perfect in weakness" (1Corinthians 12:9).NIV*

> *"For the Lord does not abandon anyone forever. Though he brings grief, he also shows compassion according to the greatness of his unfailing love. For he does not enjoy hurting people or causing them sorrow."*
> *Lamentations 3:31 NLT*

Father, thank you for being my "bridge over troubled waters" - my "hope at the end of the rope". Amen

Hold That Thought!

"We demolish arguments and every pretension that sets itself up against the knowledge of God, and we take captive every thought to make it obedient to Christ." 2 Corinthians 10:5 NIV

It starts with our thoughts! A seed of doubt, lust, envy, pride, or bitterness, begins with the thought, and takes root in our heart and then possession of our mind and our will and we allow ourselves to be overcome and dominated by sin.

> *"May he be pleased by all these thoughts about him, for I rejoice in the LORD."*
> *Psalm 104:34 NLT*

King Saul's jealousy and hatred of David sprang from hearing "Saul has killed his thousands, and David his ten thousands!" (!Samual 18:7b). David's sin with Bathsheba all started when he saw her and lusted for her.

Why do we allow ourselves to be overcome and dominated by sin, when our new birth in Christ has set us free? "For sin shall not have dominion over you, for you are not under law but under grace."(Romans 6:14).

The answer has something to do with our fleshly thoughts taking over our spiritual. When we allow our free will to choose to let those thoughts take us where we should not go, we have dropped our guard and left home without the "full armor of God."

By the power of the Holy Spirit living within the heart of every believer, we can "just say no" to the darts of evil thoughts the evil one is constantly throwing at us.

If Eve had just taken the thought to disobey God captive, we would not be having to deal with this problem today. When we realize that God is not going to give us any temptation without the grace to overcome , and without providing a means of escape from it, we can begin to filter every thought through the mind of Christ, and put the ones that don't reflect Him and His glory on permanent hold.

> *"Fix your thoughts on what is true and honorable and right."*
> *Philippians 4:8 NLT*

Father, help me to control my thoughts that the sinful ones not have their way within me. Amen

You Can't Take it With You

"If the work survives the fire, that builder will receive a reward. But if the work is burned up, the builder will suffer great loss. The builders themselves will be saved, but like someone escaping through a wall of flames." 1 Corinthians 3:14 NLT

The idea of sending ahead treasures in heaven has unjustly fallen in disrepute for far too long among many Christians. Failure to distinguish between our destination and what we will do when we get there has caused many of us to give little thought that there are rewards in heaven other than heaven itself.

> *"Moreover by them Your servant is warned, And in keeping them there is great reward."*
> *Psalm 19:11*

As St. Paul emphasizes in Ephesians 2:9 NLT*: "Salvation is not a reward for the good things we have done, so none of us can boast about it".* Scripture after Scripture attests to the fact that Heaven is our destination by grace through faith and not of works.

This being the case, why does Scripture after Scripture mention rewards in Heaven? *"Be happy about it! Be very glad! For a great reward awaits you in heaven."(Matthew 5:1). "If the master returns and finds that the servant has done a good job, there will be a reward."(Matthew 24:6). See, I am coming soon, and my reward is with me, to repay all according to their deeds" (Rev 22:12).*

And what could be better than heaven? Personally, I can't wait to find out. For those who love the Lord, to hear "Well done thou good and faithful servant" would be a great reward in itself. The prospect of getting a "good job in heaven" so that we can love the Lord even more by serving Him more would be even greater. One thing is sure: Although we can't take our time, talents, and treasures with us, we can send them ahead!

> *"but lay up for yourselves treasures in heaven, where neither moth nor rust destroys and where thieves do not break in and steal."*
> *Matthew 6:20*

Father, thank you for your free gift of heaven. Help me to do those good works here for which You created me before I was born so that I can receive the rewards that You promise. Amen

A Standard of Giving to Match Your Standard of Living
"Much is required from those to whom much is given, and much more is required from those to whom much more is given." Luke 12:48 NLT

We can say we love God all our lives, but where's the evidence? Perhaps the best answer is found in how freely we give of our time, talents, and treasures as conduits of God's love to others. St Paul says that giving *"is one way to prove your love is real."* (2:Corinthians 8:8b)

> *"Once I was young, and now I am old. Yet I have never seen the godly forsaken, nor seen their children begging for bread."*
> *Psalm 37:25 NLT*

One of the greatest robberies Satan and our flesh can ever commit is to rob us of the joy of giving. It's easy to experience this joy when we give to our spouses or family or friends, but for some reason, Satan or our flesh wants to step in and harden our hearts and pocketbooks to the Lord and others in need.

If God had responded to us the way we all too often respond to giving of any kind – graceless, condemningly, grudgingly and self centered - we would all be doomed to eternal damnation. Praise be to God, that: *"God showed his great love for us by sending Christ to die for us while we were still sinners." (Romans 5:8 NLT)*

The truth is that God does not need our time, talents, or treasures nearly as much as we need to give them. He owns them all, and just loans them out to us.

We need to be possessed by God instead of the treasures and "trivial pursuits" that all too often seem to possess us.

> *"Since you excel in so many ways—you have so much faith, such gifted speakers, such knowledge, such enthusiasm, and such love for us—now I want you to excel also in this gracious ministry of giving"*
> *2 Corinthians 8:7 NLT*

If God has blessed you with a standard of living that affords leisure time, abundant financial resources, and special talents, does your standard of giving give Him the glory for this?

Father, help my standard of giving to match my standard of living that I might glorify You and be a good and faithful steward. Amen

Practice Makes Perfect

"Keep putting into practice all you learned from me and heard from me and saw me doing, and the God of peace will be with you."
Philippians 4:9 NLT

Sometimes it seems that all we ever do is practice. We practice singing, dancing, driving, golfing, speaking. I remember having to practice what to do if my plane had to ditch in the ocean. After years of nap practice, I find that I can nap about anywhere, any place, and under any circumstances.

> *"Give me understanding and I will obey your law; I will put it into practice with all my heart."*
> *Psalm 119:34 NLT*

Most of us haven't had to go to sin practice, it just seems something that we are naturally good at. The willful and deliberate practice of a sin bears consequences for ourselves and others that we really can't afford.

When you think about it, life is really one big practice for the life that is to come for all believers in Jesus Christ.

Spiritual maturity doesn't come overnight. It takes a lot of grace, a lot of practice, and God discipline. Fortunately God knew this and gave us the Holy Spirit to help us.

Practicing prayer *"The earnest prayer of a righteous person has great power and wonderful results." (James 5:16b NLT);* abiding in the Word (He replied, *"But even more blessed are all who hear the word of God and put it into practice." (Luke 11:28);* daily dying to sin *"So you should consider yourselves dead to sin and able to live for the glory of God through Christ Jesus." (Romans 6:11);* and persevering through trials and disappointments *"But he who endures to the end shall be saved." (Matthew 24:13)* As we practice these spiritual disciplines, we begin to enjoy the "foretaste of glory" that awaits us in heaven.

> *"Whoever does not practice righteousness is not of God, nor is he who does not love his brother."*
> *1 John 3:10*

Father, Help me to practice "walking the walk" into spiritual maturity by the power of Your Spirit. Amen

Wanna Speak to the Owner?

"Do not let sin control the way you live; do not give in to its lustful desires. Do not let any part of your body become a tool of wickedness," Romans 6:12 NLT

We don't like to admit that we have an owner. "I did it my way", "Be all that YOU can be", and other songs reaffirm that it is all about us and that we are the "captains of our fate"!   And then we give up control of our lives to a pill, alchohol, lust, pride, power, idolatry or any number of other severe task masters.

> "The precepts of the LORD are right, giving joy to the heart. The commands of the LORD are radiant, giving light to the eyes."
> Psalm 19:8 NIV

Thankfully we Christians have an owner who is always ready to take calls, even collect.calls. We were bought and paid for by the blood of Jesus Christ on the Cross at Calvary, and He rightfully owns us. We no longer have to be slaves to sin, but can actually be slaves to righteousness, because God has destroyed sin's control over us and set us free from its bondage.

Our new owner has plenty to say to us. "Don't be conformed to this world, but be transformed by the renewing of your mind", "Put on the full armor of God", "Resist the devil and he will flee", "thou shalt have no other gods before me" are just a few that come to mind.

When our owner comes and asks us to give an accounting of the life that He has given us, are we going to have any fruit to show worthy of the price He paid for us?

We know that we can never be worthy, but we can surely be thankful and let our thanks be known by the fruits of righteousness which we can lay before the King. Are you ready to "speak to the owner"?

> "But God is so rich in mercy, and he loved us so very much, that even while we were dead because of our sins, he gave us life when he raised Christ from the dead."
> Ephesians 2:4,5 NLT

Father, thank you for taking ownership of me. By the power of Your Spirit, help me to do the good things You planned for me to do before I was even born. Amen

Oral Hygiene

"If you want a happy life and good days, keep your tongue from speaking evil,and keep your lips from telling lies." 1 Peter 3:10b NIV

Oral Hygiene is a mega billion dollar business world wide. We have electric toothbrushes, teeth whiteners, all sorts of mouth washes, and of course, your favorite flavor toothpaste. Which brings up an interesting question...have you ever tried to put toothpaste back into the tube?

> *"Who may worship in your sanctuary, LORD? Who may enter your presence on your holy hill? Those who lead blameless lives and do what is right, speaking the truth from sincere hearts."*
> *Psalm 15:1,2 NIV*

As impossible as that might be, it is still easier than taking back those words spoken in thoughtlessness, anger, pride, or conceit that are better left unspoken. Once out of our mouth they can kill relationships, fuel fires, and destroy our Christian witness.

As funny as some jokes might be to us, the embarrassment that comes from people being offended by their content is not funny at all.

Not only what you say, but the way you say it can be more abrasive than sandpaper and do a lot of damage. "For whatever is in your heart determines what you say. A good person produces good words from a good heart, and an evil person produces evil words from an evil heart." Matthew 12:34b,35 NLT

It is better to let an argument die from lack of fuel than to jump in and fan the flames. It still takes two to argue. There is no breath sweetener made that can match the sweetness of God's Spirit within us. "Surely it is God's Spirit within people, the breath of the Almighty within them, that makes them intelligent." Job 32:8

> *"If you claim to be religious but don't control your tongue, you are just fooling yourself, and your religion is worthless."*
> *James 1:26 NLT*

Father, help me to "clean up my act" by letting what comes out of my mouth reflect Your love, Your grace, and Your kindness. Amen

Are you Illegitimate?

"These trials are only to test your faith, to show that it is strong and pure. It is being tested as fire tests and purifies gold—and your faith is far more precious to God than mere gold" 1 Peter 1:7 NLT

I think I first heard this from Max Lucado, and if not him, I thank

> *"I know, O LORD, that your decisions are fair; you disciplined me because I needed it."*
> *Psalm 119:75 NLT*

whoever gave me this thought to ponder: "God loves you just the way you are, but too much to let you stay that way".

When we think that God promised us a rose garden in this life, we are in for some big surprises. As works in progress, we are going to find that the Lord who loves us with an everlasting love also loves us with a "tough love" and is going to do whatever it takes to conform us into the image of His Son.

The slower we learn that God's ways are really the best ways for living the abundant, fulfilling life on this earth, the more mistakes, heartaches, and needless pain we are going to have to endure before we learn to totally abide in Him.

Although we are no longer bound to the law for salvation, the Holy Spirit still uses the law to convict us of our sins, and as a guide and a curb. Whenever we overstep the boundaries of the law, we can fully expect that God will give us whatever degree of reproof, chastening, or scourging He deems necessary to bring us back onto the path of righteousness.

Does this mean that we should respond in anger or by doubting God's love when we experience God's chastening? Does it mean that we should go "eat a worm and die" in self pity? Of course not!

> *"If God doesn't discipline you as he does all of his children, it means that you are illegitimate and are not really his children after all"*
> *Hebrews 12:8 NLT*

We should respond by 1. Rejoicing in God's love 2. Repenting 3. Moving on!.

Father, by the power of your Holy Spirit, give me a faith that will not fail, a hope that will not disappear, and Your all sufficient grace to see me through Your process of conforming me into the image of Jesus. Amen

"Itchy" Ears?

"For the time will come when they will not endure sound doctrine, but according to their own desires, because they have itching ears, they will heap up for themselves teachers; and they will turn their ears away from the truth, and be turned aside to fables" 2 Timothy 4:3,4

There is a great epidemic of "ear itch" going on throughout the world. Many have become completely deaf, and even worse, others have misinterpreted God's Word into fables that make "Alice in Wonderland" more believable.

> *"Listen, for I will speak of excellent things, and from the opening of my lips will come right things; for my mouth will speak truth;"*
> *Proverbs 8:6,7a*

Truth has become relative truth, the 10 commandments have become the ten suggestions, marriage has been redefined to include those of the same sex, and sin has become an irrelevant word. Many hear what they want to hear and choose to ignore or spin what we don't want to hear in the name of tolerance, women's rights, gay rights, or a mistaken concept of love.

God makes it very clear *"that no prophecy of Scripture is of any private interpretation, for prophecy never came by the will of man, but holy men of God spoke as they were moved by the Holy Spirit." (2 Peter 1:20).* "All Scripture is given by inspiration of God, and is profitable for doctrine, for reproof, for correction, for instruction in righteousness," (1 Timothy 3:16)

> *"For the hearts of these people are hardened, and their ears cannot hear, and they have closed their eyes—so their eyes cannot see, and their ears cannot hear, and their hearts cannot understand, and they cannot turn to me and let me heal them."*
> *Matthew 13:15 NLT*

If we would know truth, we had better get to know Jesus and what He stands for, or we are apt to fall for anything that our "itchy ears" hear through the world, the flesh, and the devil.

Have you checked your hearing lately?

Father, thank you for giving me the Holy Spirit so that my eyes can see, my ears can hear, and my mind can comprehend. Amen

Are You "World Class"?
"And do not be conformed to this world, but be transformed by the renewing of your mind, that you may prove what is that good and acceptable and perfect will of God." Romans 12:2

We often hear "world class" used to describe outstanding athletes, orchestras, tourist attractions, as being among the best in the world.

> *"In this life they consider themselves fortunate, and the world loudly applauds their success"*
> *Psalm 49:18 NLT*

The problem is that the world's standards of morality and life have deteriorated so badly that it is producing "world class" sinners.

Satan is doing everything possible to get us to "curse God and die" like the rest of the world. As the world comes into our homes through TV, the internet, and newspapers, we are targeted from the age of 3 to find our needs satisfaction in the latest toy, cartoon, beer, or perfume.

The Christian faith and lifestyle is constantly being challenged and undermined in so many subtle and not so subtle ways it takes all the spiritual discernment and strength from the Holy Spirit we can get to keep from being sucked into the cesspool of the world view.

Family values have been undermined for 2 generations on TV shows showing dads as idiots and God as a butt of jokes. Now TV shows are blatantly flaunting homosexuality, fornication, greed, and idolatry of every kind as the "world class" standard for living, loving, and finding true happiness. Does the one with the most toys really win?

> *"For all that is in the world—the lust of the flesh, the lust of the eyes, and the pride of life—is not of the Father but is of the world."*
> *1 John 2:16*

In a world obsessed with sex and materialism, the call to living holy, "set apart" lives is falling more and more on deaf ears, but to those who claim Jesus Christ as Lord and Savior, it's a call to becoming saints who are still the salt and the light of the world.

Father, let me not fall in love with my self or the world. Let me be transformed into the image of Christ. Amen

29

Have You Ordered Yours?

"Most assuredly, I say to you, if anyone keeps My word he shall never see death." John 8:51 NIV

There is a relative new "bon voyage" gift that you can buy for yourself

> *"I will abide in Your tabernacle forever; I will trust in the shelter of Your wings"*
> *Psalm 61:4*

or tell your loved ones you to get it for you.. You can get one to express the passion of your life, or your proudness in your alma mater. You can attend your going away party in a Commemorative Casket!

Commemorative Memorials in Macon Georgia have licensing rights from most colleges to use the school colors and seal on caskets, and now die hard fans and alums can express their admiration for their college or university right up to the end. (Nebraska Cornhusker and Tennesee Volunteer fans have so far been the best customers).

Actually, we shouldn't spend too much or worry at all about caskets, because we are not going to be there! I died and was buried when I was baptized. This new life that we have through faith in Jesus Christ is eternal life, which means we are going to live forever! *"I tell you the truth, whoever hears my word and believes him who sent me has eternal life and will not be condemned; he has crossed over from death to life."(John 5:24 NLT)*

When we have completed God's purposes and we leave this corruptible body behind, our spirits will be instantly transported into the presence of God! "I tell you the truth, today you will be with me in paradise" (Luke 23:43). There we will wait for our new bodies at the "resurrection of the just."

Frankly, rather than spending money on a commemorative casket, I would rather have it spent on a great praise band and dinner party. For the believer, death is not the end of anything, but the beginning of everything! And that's cause for real celebration!

> *"How we thank God, who gives us victory over sin and death through Jesus Christ our Lord!"*
> *1 Corinthians 15:57 NLT*

Father, thank you for giving me the faith to know that because You live I can face all the tomorrows with Your joy in this life and in eternity. Amen

The Pearl of Great Price

"When he discovered a pearl of great value, he sold everything he owned and bought it! " Matthew 13:46 NLT

In some ways, life can be likened to one big treasure hunt. Since the beginning of time, man has been searching for the meaning and purposes of life with many not even coming close to the answer.

> *"I rejoice in Your word like one who finds a great treasure."*
> *Psalm 119:162 NLT*

Although God has put it into the heart of every man to know Him, and fills all creation with evidence of His existence, man continues to look for treasure in all the wrong places and eventually comes up empty handed.

Whether seeking gratification and validation of ones self through the approval of others, power, fame or fortune; or through dancing to the world's tune we wander aimlessly lost until we find that real treasure.

In asking ourselves "what is my pearl of great price" just ask where or with whom do we spend the greatest amount of our time. How do we spend the greatest amount of our discretionary resources? How do we use our talents that are on loan from God? What do we possess and what possesses us?

The rich young ruler was at least honest enough to walk away because he was possessed by his riches.

When we leave this world, we are leaving just as we came in, naked as jaybirds and without any of the treasures we held so dear and qualities we treasured so much – unless we are leaving with that "pearl of great price" which is our salvation through faith in Jesus Christ. Do you really dare to leave "home" without this?

> *"the ransom he paid was not mere gold or silver. He paid for you with the precious lifeblood of Christ, the sinless, spotless Lamb of God."*
> *1 Peter 1:18b.19 NLT*

Father, Help me to hold on to the real pearl of life eternal life by the power of Your Holy Spirit. Amen.

Are You Underinsured?

"Because He has appointed a day on which He will judge the world in righteousness by the Man whom He has ordained. He has given assurance of this to all by raising Him from the dead." Acts 17:31

You can insure about any possible risk. From the unlikely possibility that someone will make a hole in one in a contest, to death policies are available. Often we never know how good our insurance is until we have to use it.

> *"My God is my rock, in whom I find protection. He is my shield, the strength of my salvation, and my stronghold, my high tower, my Savior, the one who saves me from violence."*
> *2 Samuel 22:3 NLT*

Sun Life Assurance of Canada is one of the giants of the insurance world, but even they cannot guarantee that losses and calamities will not happen, but only that they will reimburse you if they do.

There is only one insurer that has never failed to honor a claim, has no hidden exceptions and will even guarantee to cover pre existing conditions. I like to call this "Son Life".

"Son Life" is the only insurance available that does not pay death benefits because "Son Life" guarantees that you will never die! The lump sum one time premium was paid for you on the Cross of Calvary when Jesus Christ gave up His life so that you could have one forever.

The application for this eternal life insurance is as simple as ABC, and cannot be rejected or cancelled. All you have to do to become fully insured is Admit that you are a sinner, Believe in the life, death, and resurrection of Jesus Christ as payment and proof of payment for your sins, and Confess this admission and belief to God and to others do not have this policy, you are seriously underinsured! Call "Son Life" or a designated representative today!

> *"let us draw near with a true heart in full assurance of faith, having our hearts sprinkled from an evil conscience and our bodies washed with pure water"*
> *Hebrews 10:22*

Father, thank you for the assurance of eternal life I have through faith in Jesus Christ. Amen

To God Be the Glory!

"But we all, with unveiled face, beholding as in a mirror the glory of the Lord, are being transformed into the same image from glory to glory, just as by the Spirit of the Lord." 2 Corinthians 3:18

"Glory" is an interesting word, appearing in Scripture well over 300

> **'Give to the LORD the glory he deserves!"**
> **Chronicles 16:19a NLT**

times. It is used to mean honor, dignity, splendor, brightness, majesty, adoration, praise, the bliss of heaven, and perhaps most importantly, the infinite perfections of God.

God chose to be born in a stable instead of a palace in order to manifest His glory. He chose a rag tag group of men of low estate rather than kings or princes to spread the gospel as proof that this was the work of God and not men.

Today, God uses ordinary people to accomplish extraordinary tasks that only God can do, lest He be robbed of His glory.

We must never lose sight of the fact that God "humbles the proud and gives grace to the humble".

Few things corrupt as much as power or pride. When we get to thinking more highly of ourselves than we ought, we become virtually useless to God.

God requires a broken spirit and a contrite heart before He can fill it with His grace and power to accomplish His purposes. David, the prodigal son, and Peter personify this truth.

It is only when we become Christ centered instead of self centered, and focus on glorifying God instead of ourselves that God's glory for which he created us can be manifested in our lives.

> **"I brought glory to you here on earth by doing everything you told me to do".**
> **John 17:4 NLT**

Father, keep me ever mindful that it's not about glorifying me, but about glorifying You. To You, alone, be all glory. Amen.

Be Careful What You Pray

"Father, if you are willing, please take this cup of suffering away from me. Yet I want your will, not mine." Luke 22:40 NLT

To pray that the Lord's will be done is one of the easiest prayers

> *"Listen to my cry for help, my King and my God, for I will never pray to anyone but you"*
> *Psalm 5:3 NLT*

to pray and yet the hardest prayer to really mean..

When we learn the secret of abiding in Him and His Word most every prayer we pray will be based on our understanding of His will and His purposes. We need to learn to submit our petitions by praying as our Lord Jesus did - that it might please God to grant our requests, but always that they be subject to His good and gracious will.

It is great to know that we have the Holy Spirit continually praying for us. *"For we don't even know what we should pray for, nor how we should pray. But the Holy Spirit prays for us with groanings that cannot be expressed in words. And the Father who knows all hearts knows what the Spirit is saying, for the Spirit pleads for us believers in harmony with God's own will." (Romans 8:26,27 NLT)*

I am forever grateful to Dr. Charles Stanley, who many years ago asked that we pray this prayer from Colossians for him. It has become the center point of all my prayers for all those I love and those I pray for. To me it is one of the best prayers in the Bible.

> *"For this reason we also, since the day we heard it, do not cease to pray for you, and to ask that you may be filled with the knowledge of His will in all wisdom and spiritual understanding; that you may walk worthy of the Lord, fully pleasing Him, being fruitful in every good work and increasing in the knowledge of God; strengthened with all might, according to His glorious power, for all patience and longsuffering with joy;"*
> *Colossians 1:9-11*

Father, help me to pray not from repetition or habit, but with real sincerity and meaning in what I pray. Amen

Things God Can't Do

"Let no one say when he is tempted, "I am tempted by God"; for God cannot be tempted by evil, nor does He Himself tempt anyone. 14But each one is tempted when he is drawn away by his own desires and enticed." James 1:13

As we proclaim the sovereignty and power of God it is easy to lose sight of one of the great truths and great comforts of our faith. There are some things God can't do!

> "I have known from my earliest days that your decrees never change."
> Psalm 119:152 NLT

God cannot be tempted by evil. He is the only one who had the power to overcome evil not for Himself, but for us, that we might be conformed to the image of Christ.

God can't lie! His every Word is truth, and we can take whatever he says or promises to the bank. *"God is not a man, that he should lie. He is not a human, that he should change his mind." (Numbers 23:19)*

God can't trust us! *"If God cannot trust his own angels and has charged some of them with folly, how much less will he trust those made of clay" (Job 4:18)* God knows the weakness of our flesh and our inability to save ourselves. This is why He sent His Son to do for us what we could not do for ourselves - be our Savior.

God can't turn His back on us! *"But this is the LORD'S reply: I would no more reject my people than I would change my laws of night and day, of earth and sky. (Jeremiah 33:25)*

Isn't it thrilling to know that we have a God who is love, who cannot fail, and in whom we can trust in every area of our lives. If you have not yet come to this realization, think about it, pray about it, and claim this reality by faith. It's true!

> "God also bound himself with an oath, so that those who received the promise could be perfectly sure that he would never change his mind."
> Hebrews 6:17 NLT

Father, I am so glad that You are my one constant in a sea of turmoil and change. Keep me anchored deep in You and Your unfailing love. Amen

The Fear is Gone

"And the fear of you and the dread of you shall be on every beast of the earth, on every bird of the air, on all that move on the earth, and on all the fish of the sea. They are given into your hand."Gen 9:2

Banff, British Columbia is an interesting place. It is moose infested! Moose have taken over the parks and the streets. They have lost the dread of humans. People can get hurt by these big animals with gigantic horns.

> *"But your iniquities have separated you from your God; And your sins have hidden His face from you, So that He will not hear"*
> *Isaiah 59:2*

Alligator attacks are on the increase in Florida. As residential developments gobble up land surrounding lakes and canals, and fisherman, water skiers, and swimmers abound in the water, there is no place for the gators to run and hide, so they lose their fear and begin looking at humans as gator bait..

The main reason that rogue alligators, moose, dogs, and other animals that attack humans are hunted down and killed is that once they lose their fear of humans, they will always be extremely dangerous.

One of the biggest causes of moral degeneration and the ever increasing problems that this causes in our society is that many people have lost their fear of God. As people willfully sin and seemingly get away with it, they become emboldened and throw off all restraints until their lives become walking cesspools of unrestrained evil.

God is mocked, treated irreverently and irrelevantly and the moral meltdown has become a river of horrors. From "sparing the rod and spoiling the child", to casting off all sexual morality and inhibitions, to promoting secular humanism that denies the reality of hell and the omnipotence of God; we are becoming a pagan society.

> *"But these, like natural brute beasts made to be caught and destroyed, speak evil of the things they do not understand, and will utterly perish in their own corruption"*
> *2 Peter 2:12*

Revival is our only hope of avoiding the fate of Sodom and Gomorroh. Let it begin within me!

Father, have mercy upon us. Let the fire of a great awakening and restoration spread throughout the world. Amen.

Webster Has Been Bridged!

"For I know the plans I have for you," declares the LORD , "plans to prosper you and not to harm you, plans to give you hope and a future." Jeremiah 29:11 NIV

I am happy to report that Webster's New Dictionary is no longer unabridged! The Lord has given me a new word that should be in every one's vocabulary and all dictionaries. This word can change your perspective and give you a whole new way of living. The new word is blessatunity, and it means "the opportunity to give or receive a blessing"

> *"Blessed is the man who fears the LORD, who delights greatly in His commandments"*
> *Psalm 112:1*

While we are looking for opportunities to advance our careers, our own agendas, and our standing among our peers; we often miss out on the opportunity for a blessing that might be found in not only the best but even in the worst of circumstances.

God's Word abounds on how we might enjoy blessatunities. We find blessed, bless, etc. almost 300 times in the Bible, and Jesus Himself tells how to be blessed over 20 times starting with the beatitudes. *"Blessed are those servants whom the master, when he comes, will find watching."* *(Luke 12:37)*, and *"But He said, "More than that, blessed are those who hear the word of God and keep it!" (Luke 11:28)*, are a couple of my personal favorites.

Is your glass half empty or half full? Do you respond to problems by self pity or by looking for what possible blessing might be there? Do you know what God's idea of blessings are? His ways are higher than our ways, and His thoughts are beyond our comprehension.

> *"Blessed are the pure in heart, for they shall see God."*
> *Matthew 5:8*

This is where faith comes in. God says that when we rejoice, are thankful, and pray, we will be blessed with that "peace that surpasses all understanding." Blessatunities are all around us! Would someone please call Mr. Webster?

Father, help me to be sensitive to the blessatunities that you provide on a daily basis and bless me so that I can be a blessing to others. Amen

Are You Down?

"With my authority, take this message of repentance to all the nations, beginning in Jerusalem: 'there is forgiveness of sins for all who turn to me." Luke 24:47 NLT

You may have never tasted goose before. But, if you are like me, you

> *"For all this His anger is not turned away, But His hand is stretched out still" Isaiah 5:25b*

have cooked plenty of them. I don't know where the expression "your goose is cooked" came from, but I know that the ones I have cooked sure left a bad after taste.

As Isaiah lists the sins of the children of Israel, he is hitting too close for comfort upon the sins of all of us today. Of all the things that never change, the sinful nature of man seems to repeat the same sins over and over, generation to generation.

The good news is that while we can never uncook a goose, we can feather our guilt and sorrow with the "down" of God's grace and become "upward bound" through faith in the life, death, and resurrection of Jesus Christ.

Goose down is much more popular than goose meat. Down filled pillows, jackets, and comforters command a premium price, and at one time, goose down feather beds were prized for sleeping comfort.

The next time you feel like "your goose is cooked" be sorry, but not discouraged. Throw yourself upon the "featherbed" of God's throne of grace with Godly sorrow and true repentance. Remember that there is no condemnation for those who are in Christ, but only restoration and all sufficient grace and mercy which are renewed every day for those who come with a broken spirit and contrite heart. *"When you bow down before the Lord and admit your dependence on Him, He will lift you up and give you honor." (James 4:10)*

> *"And do not bring sorrow to God's Holy Spirit by the way you live. Remember, He is the one who has identified you as His own, guaranteeing that you will be saved on the day of redemption" Ephesians 4:30 NLT*

Father, thank You for taking the cup of death for the wages of sin away from me by sending Jesus to die for my sins on the cross at Calvary. Amen

38

Worlds Worst Motivational Word

"The sinful mind is hostile to God. It does not submit to God's law, nor can it do so. Those controlled by the sinful nature cannot please God." Romans 8:7,8 NIV

"Don't" is one of the first words we have trouble understanding as children. We usually have to get spanked, scolded, or hurt several times before we realize that it means "do not" instead of "do".

> *"But the man who looks intently into the perfect law that gives freedom, and continues to do this, not forgetting what he has heard, but doing it – he will be blessed in what he does,"*
> *James 1:25 NIV*

We feel compelled to walk on the grass, touch the wet paint, park, lust, envy, and respond by doing exactly what we are told or asked not to do. Getting a movie banned somewhere most always assures it being a big hit.

God recognized our problem and has provided a cure. His name is Jesus!

It is only by the grace of God in sending His Son to die on the cross for our sins, and through the power of the Holy Spirit that we can do the "do's" and don't the "don'ts". When we receive Jesus Christ as our Savior, we are "new creatures" and under new management.

Because of what He has done for us, we want to do the things He wants us to do, and we no longer are compelled to do the things He forbids. Although we may momentarily stumble and fall back into our old nature from time to time, we can be sure that God is at work in us through the indwelling presence of the Holy Spirit to cleanse and conform us into the mind of Christ on an ongoing, daily basis when we daily die to sin and become alive in Christ through daily confession and repentance.

> *"But now, by dying to what once bound us, we have been released from the law so that we serve in the new way of the Spirit, and not in the old way of the written code."*
> *Romans 7:6 NIV*

Father, help me to do the "do's" and don't the "don'ts" by the power of Your Spirit living in me. Amen

Saint or Sinner?

"Taste and see that the LORD is good; blessed is the man who takes refuge in Him. Fear the LORD, you his saints, for those who fear Him lack nothing. [1]The lions may grow weak and hungry, but those who seek the LORD lack no good thing.." Psalm 34:8-10 NIV

We have a tendency to undervalue the wonderful inheritance that we

> *"I will listen to what God the LORD will say; He promises peace to his people, His saints- but let them not return to folly."*
> *Psalm 85.8 NIV*

have when we by faith in Jesus Christ became joint heirs with Him. We become dead to sin and alive in Christ. We receive all of the rights of sonship, which means that we have been sanctified and made holy in the sight of God and have become Saints in the household of faith.

There are times that we don't feel like saints. There are certainly times that we don't act like saints. Thank God, our sainthood is not based on our feelings or performance, but on the performance of Jesus Christ in dying on the cross for us, so that we could be reconciled to God and become saints in His eyes. We need to understand that there are two types of sin. One has to do with our inherited curse of sin, the other with our sinful actions..

When we accept or accepted Jesus Christ as our Savior, our standing with God changed from sinner to saint. We are set free from the bondage of sin, *"Therefore, there is no condemnation for those who are in Christ Jesus" (Romans 8:1)* We are no longer miserable sinners, but redeemed saints!

In spite of our new position as saints, many of our actions are often sinful. We should be ashamed, sorry; and then confess and repent of them. We can be sure that God is at work in us, perfecting us into the image of Christ and we are going to be like Him someday.

> *"Praise be to the God and Father of our Lord Jesus Christ, who has blessed us in the heavenly realms with every spiritual blessing in Christ. For he chose us in him before the creation of the world to be holy and blameless in his sight."*
> *Ephesians 1:3 NIV*

Father, thank you for who I am in You! By the power of Your Spirit, let me live like it. Amen

You're a Winner!

"Therefore, as God's chosen people, holy and dearly loved, clothe yourselves with compassion, kindness, humility, gentleness and patience." Colossians 3:12 NIV

There is hardly a day goes by that I do not find that I have won something! My mail comes with envelopes proclaiming "you're a winner".

> *"Now I know that the LORD saves his anointed; He answers him from His holy heaven*
> *with the saving power of His right hand."*
> *Psalm 20:6 NIV*

All I have to do is go down to the car dealer"s and pick up one of 5 prizes.

My internet is filled with pop ups declaring me a winner. I have won more "3 free nights for 2 in Orlando" than I can remember.

There has been quite a dialogue going on within the body of Christ for several centuries now about the sovereignty of God vs. the freedom of the will. One thing is certain. We were dead in trespasses and sin and dead men have no power or will to do anything. It takes the grace of God exercised through His sovereign will to give any of us our life in Christ.

As scripture plainly says: *"So I want you to know how to discern what is truly from God: No one speaking by the Spirit of God can curse Jesus, and no one is able to say, "Jesus is Lord," except by the Holy Spirit." (1 Corinthians 12:3)*

The bottom line is that if you truly believe in Jesus Christ as your Savior and Lord, you are one of God's elect. He has selected you, He will continually inspect you, correct you, protect you, and perfect you more and more into the image of His son. You're a winner! Start living and running the race of life like one!

> *"Who will bring any charge against those whom God has chosen? It is God who justifies."*
> *Romans 8:33 NIV*

Father, thank you for calling me by name and making me one of Your very own by Your grace. Amen.

41

Trophies of God's Grace

"But you are a chosen people, a royal priesthood, a holy nation, a people belonging to God, that you may declare the praises of him who called you out of darkness into his wonderful light." 1Peter 2:9 NIV

We are humbled when we think of all the heroes of the faith and saints

> "But the eyes of the LORD are on those who fear Him, on those whose hope is in His unfailing love,"
> Psalm 33:8 NIV

who are the trophies of Gods grace. By faith Abraham was willing to kill his own son as a sacrifice to God, believing that God could raise him from the dead. Joseph overcame slavery and prison, and St Paul was determined to wipe out Christians from the face of the earth thinking he was in God's will.

The truth that we too are trophies of God's grace and priests may seem a frightening concept. We certainly don't always live like priests, and we surely don't look like a trophy.

. As trophies of God's grace we have to consider whether we are mindful of the price that was paid for our sainthood, and whether we are living in a manner that reflects who we are in Christ.

Fortunately for us, our being trophies does not depend on our behavior, but on the behavior of Jesus Christ on the Cross at Calvary. But, at the very least, we should always seek God's power through the Holy Spirit to walk in the wonderful light of God's love, doing the good works that He prepared for us even before we were born.

> "These were all commended for their faith, yet none of them received what had been promised. 40God had planned something better for us so that only together with us would they be made perfect."
> Hebrews 11:39 NIV

When we consider the price that was paid for us, we should give even more thought to how we might respond to God's love and undeserved favor as trophies of His grace.

Father keep me ever mindful of who I am in You, and help me to live like it. Amen

Take This Job and Love it!

"And whatever you do, whether in word or deed, do it all in the name of the Lord Jesus, giving thanks to God the Father through him." Colossians 3:17 NIV

Don't you just love to see people who love their work and are really good at it? Isn't it sad to see people trapped in jobs they hate and have no ability for? When possible, we should leave it or otherwise ask God to give us the grace to help us cope with it from His perspective.

> *"May the favor of the Lord our God rest upon us; establish the work of our hands for us - yes, establish the work of our hands."*
> *Psalm 90:17 NIV*

As Christians we must understand *"For we are God's workmanship, created in Christ Jesus to do good works, which God prepared in advance for us to do. (Ephesians 2:10).* Good stewardship of the life we have been given demands that we devote our time, talents, and resources for God's purposes as well as for our own. God has equipped us all differently for different tasks. We need always to check our equipment and use our best talents in serving the Lord.

Especially in serving God with our time and talents, we need to know that serving under compulsion and guilt are not good enough. God not only loves a cheerful giver of money, but also expects our gift of time and talents to be given in the joy of the Lord without complaining or feeling put upon.

It is when we look at our jobs from God's perspective that we can learn to love them more. When we realize work is a blessing, and that we are actually working to please God, it can make a big difference on how much we love our jobs in the church and in the workplace. .

> *"Serve wholeheartedly, as if you were serving the Lord, not men"*
> *Ephesians 3:17*

Father, thank you for the talents you have given me. Help me to use them to glorify You in Your church and in the workplace. Amen.

World's Champion!

"Even youths will become exhausted, and young men will give up. But those who wait on the LORD will find new strength. They will fly high on wings like eagles. They will run and not grow weary. They will walk and not faint. Isaiah 30:40 NLT

It has just dawned upon me that I am probably a World's Champion! Good as it sounds, it is not always something to brag about.

> *"Think about all He endured when sinful people did such terrible things to Him, so that you don't become weary and give up"*
> *Hebrews 12:3 NLT*

In my case, I have done it in Florida, North Carolina, South Carolina, Virginia, West Virginia, Maryland, Indiana and Kentucky. I have done it in Cadillacs, Lincolns, Volvo's, Dodges, Fords, and several other makes. I am here and now laying title for the dubious distinction of being the World's Champion gas "runner outer!"

I don't know what part about "empty" on the gas gauge I don't seem to understand. The tendency I have to only fill up at a filling station on the side of the road I'm traveling has also been partly to blame.

. I have survived running out of gas literally, and by the grace of God, and by the power of the Holy Spirit have been protected from "running out of gas" spiritually for most of my life.

Just as gasoline is fuel for the automobile, the Word of God is fuel for the soul. We are told to be filled with the Spirit so that we don't obey the lusts of the flesh. We are told that we have been given the indwelling of the Holy Spirit God's guarantee that He will give us everything He has promised (Ephesians 4:1), and, best of all: *"being confident of this very thing, that He who has begun a good work in you will complete it until the day of Jesus Christ;" (Philippians 1:6)* Need a fill up?

> *" Are pressed on every side by troubles, but we are not crushed and broken. We are perplexed, but we don't give up and quit"*
> *2 Corinthians 4:8 NLT*

Father, thank you for Your promise that You will never run out of patience with me, even when I seem to be running low on you. Amen.

All Prisoners are not in Prison

"Jesus answered them, "Most assuredly, I say to you, whoever commits sin is a slave of sin. And a slave does not abide in the house forever, *but* a son abides forever. Therefore if the Son makes you free, you shall be free indeed." John 8:34

There are some convicted felons in prison freer than many people living in the outside world. They have that

> *"The LORD frees the prisoners. The LORD opens the eyes of the blind."*
> **Psalm 146.7b,8**

peace and joy that only comes to the truly free while many on the outside are in captivity to all sorts things.

Sometimes the walls we build around us to keep others out seem to imprison us by keeping us withdrawn and missing out on so much of God's love that is all around us. There are denominational, racial, and relational walls that need to come down.

It is a terrible thing to be captured and held hostage by an addiction of any kind that takes control of our lives and imprisons us. Whether its guilt, addiction to drugs, alcohol, or pornography, the consequences can be crushing not only to us but to those we love.

The good news is that there is a cure available. Jesus said: "'The Spirit of the Lord is upon me, for He has appointed me to preach Good News to the poor. He has sent me to proclaim that captives will be released, that the blind will see, that the downtrodden will be freed from their oppressors, and that the time of the Lord's favor has come." (Luke 4:18). Saint Paul tells us to bring every thought into captivity into obedience to Christ.

Before coming to faith in Jesus Christ there was no cure for sin available. Now that we have been set free from the power of sin to destroy us spiritually, we need to allow the Holy Spirit to take control of our lives so that sin might have no dominion over us.

> *"Likewise you also, reckon yourselves to be dead indeed to sin, but alive to God in Christ Jesus our Lord."*
> **Romans 6:11**

Father, come into my life and take charge that I no longer be a slave to sin, but to Your righteousness. Amen.

Who's in Your Closet?

"Those who worship false gods turn their backs on all God's mercies. But I will offer sacrifices to you with songs of praise, and I will fulfill all my vows. For my salvation comes from the LORD alone."Jonah 2:8 NLT

Worship is much much more than a formal ceremony at some church on Sunday. Worship is the ongoing every day praise of God through the sacrifice of giving our time, talents, treasures, and submitting to His will for our lives.

> *"Sing to the LORD; bless His name. Each day proclaim the good news that He saves."*
> *Psalm 96:2 NLT*

Sometimes, in spite of our best intentions, we get so preoccupied with the cares of this world and other distractions we tend to put God in the closet every Sunday along with our "go to meeting clothes", and spend the rest of the week taking on the world, the flesh and the devil in our own strength. This is a recipe for disaster.

God doesn't belong in the closet in your house, He belongs in the closet of your heart, where He can "stick closer than a brother", guiding you into all righteousness and revealing all truth.

When the love of God and His Spirit fills your heart, your worship will flow like rivers of living water into the lives of those around you. If He is left in the clothes closet, your heart has a tendency to be filled with the idols of your flesh and you are an easy prey for the evil one who is out to destroy.

There is also no room in the kingdom of God for "closet Christians" who hoard their faith and God's love and pass up every opportunity to confess Jesus to others. *"Therefore whoever confesses Me before men, him I will also confess before My Father who is in heaven. But whoever denies Me before men, him I will also deny before My Father who is in heaven".* (Matthew 10:32 NLT)

> *"But the time is coming and is already here when true worshipers will worship the Father in spirit and in truth. The Father is looking for anyone who will worship Him that way."*
> *John 4:23 NLT*

Father, forgive me for putting You in the wrong closet too many times. Help me to come out of the closet and bring You with me. Amen

Anchor Deep!

"This confidence is like a strong and trustworthy anchor for our souls. It leads us through the curtain of heaven into God's inner sanctuary. Jesus has already gone in there for us. He has become our eternal High Priest in the line of Melchizedek." Hebrews 6:19 NLT

"Through many dangers, toils, and snares I have already come, 'tis grace hath brought me safe thus far, and grace will lead me home". No wonder "Amazing Grace" is perhaps the most beloved and often sung hymn of all time!

> *"I am holding you by your right hand—I, the LORD your God. And I say to you, 'Do not be afraid. I am here to help you."*
>
> *Isaiah 41:13 NLT*

Our lives can be likened to a voyage on the sea. We go through still waters, and some really rough storms. Ships have anchors to help ride out the rough seas and we have God's Word. The deeper we anchor into God's Word, the better able we become to ride out the storms of life.

Here are some samples of the strength and assurances we find in God's Word: *"God is our refuge and strength, always ready to help in times of trouble."(Psalm 46:1 NLT). "What do you mean, 'If I can'?" Jesus asked. "Anything is possible if a person believes". (Mark 9:23 NLT). "For He has not ignored the suffering of the needy. He has not turned and walked away. He has listened to their cries for help."(Psalm 22:24 NLT) "But the LORD still waits for you to come to him so he can show you his love and compassion. For the LORD is a faithful God. Blessed are those who wait for him to help them".(Isaiah 20:18 NLT).* The more we "anchor deep" into God's Word the more power and strength we receive from it to ride out the storms of life.

Our strength may fail, people will often fail us, and our possessions may all disappear. When we are tossed about with "many a conflict and many a doubt" we need Jesus, "the author and perfector of our faith", the anchor of our souls.

> *"For I can do everything with the help of Christ who gives me the strength I need."*
>
> *Philippians 4:13 NLT*

Father, thank you for the grace that You have promised that is sufficient for all our needs. Help me to "anchor deep". Amen

47

Is God Fair?

"He is entirely fair and just in this present time when he declares sinners to be right in his sight because they believe in Jesus" Romans 3:26 NLT

If beauty is in the eye of the beholder, fairness is often in the eye of the

> *"For I was envious of the boastful, When I saw the prosperity of the wicked"*
> *Psalm 73:3*

self interested. Whether criticizing referees' calls against our favorite team, or complaining about someone making more money than us, or getting promoted over us, "it's not fair" is often one of the most subjective judgments we ever make.

Many books have been written about the fairness of bad things happening to good people, and many people have been estranged from God over their anger of what they perceive to be unfair treatment by God.

We need to remember several things before we rush to judgment about the fairness of God. First of all, we must recognize that God is sovereign and we are His to do with as He pleases. Secondly, we need to remember that God's ways are higher than our understanding. We also need to remember that often in "working all things to the good" of those who love Him, God uses discipline, chastening, and sometimes bad things in order to conform us into the image of His Son.

Before we go down the road questioning the fairness of God, we need to remember that if God were fair, we would all be bound for hell. We have all sinned and fallen short of the glory of God, and our personal righteousness is as filthy rags.

> *"I wish to give to this last man the same as to you. Is it not lawful for me to do what I wish with my own things?"*
> *Matthew 20:14b.15*

Thank God that He is not fair, but full of grace and mercy. Do we dare bring God's fairness into question?

Father, let me never trade the assurances I have in Your grace and mercy for the consequences I would suffer if You were fair. Amen

Put on the Blinkers!

"Let your eyes look straight ahead, and your eyelids look right before you. Ponder the path of your feet, and let all your ways be established. Do not turn to the right or the left; remove your foot from evil." Proverbs 4:25

Some race horses get so frightened by crowds that they slow down as they head for home and the big crowds awaiting. Others get so distracted by horses coming up beside them they tend to slow down, veer to fight, or just worry about them.

> "But my eyes are upon You, O GOD the Lord; in You I take refuge; do not leave my soul destitute."
> *Psalm 141.8*

Blinkers are cups worn around the eyes of horses to cut down their line of vision to avoid these fears and distractions that impede their running the race, and they have turned many losers into winners.

Rather than "pluck out the eye" that causes us to sin, perhaps we should just "put on the blinkers" and shut out the distractions and fears that are slowing down our progress in the race of life.

When we turn our eyes upon Jesus, "the author and perfector of our faith" we are focused on what really matters. When our relationship is right with Him, we have the power of the Holy Spirit to overcome the power of sin and temptation to slow us down.

When we major in the major focus on seeking the kingdom of God first, everything else we need is added. The victor's prize is the crown of righteousness that has already been laid up for us in heaven.

In horse racing, there is a big bonus awaiting the horse that wins the triple crown. In the kingdom of God, heaven is not a reward but a gift which we receive by faith.

The reward is what we earn by being obedient and being fruitful in the good works for which we were created. When we shut out the distractions we are well on our way to winning the God's double crown of grace and reward.

> "Follow the Lord's rules for doing his work, just as an athlete either follows the rules or is disqualified and wins no prize."
> *2 Timothy 2:5 NLT*

Father, by the power of Your Spirit, help me to shut out the distractions and stay focused on running for Your "well done".Amen

49

Wandering Aimlessly Lost

"So my people are wandering like lost sheep, without a shepherd to protect and guide them." Zechariah 10:2b NLT

Although painful, those of us who know what it was like to "wander aimlessly lost" need to sometimes revisit the futility of our lives and the emptiness of our hearts before the Lord found us and called us into saving faith and the abundant life we have in Him.

> *"Some wandered in the desert, lost and homeless. Hungry and thirsty, they nearly died. "LORD, help!" they cried in their trouble,and he rescued them from their distress."*
> *Psalm 107:4-6 NLT*

Thinking about our past should give us even greater passion to seek out and save the lost living among us in our homes, our workplace, and in our everyday lives. It should also trigger a daily wellspring of praise to the Lord of salvation and the great thing He has done for us.

People today need the Lord as never before. The "household god" called TV has mislead and brainwashed two generations of people with so many lies about what constitutes the good life, and what really matters. No wonder there is so much misery and sin all around us.

Broken homes, suicide rates, and addictions of every kind have made the age of secular humanism a vast wasteland of broken hearts, shattered dreams, wasted lives and unfilled expectations for millions.

> *"My dear brothers and sisters, if anyone among you wanders away from the truth and is brought back again, you can be sure that the one who brings that person back will save that sinner from death and bring about the forgiveness of many sins."*
> *James 5:19,20 NLT*

Through it all, we have a God who still loves us , who would have all men to be saved and who would use us to seek out and proclaim the good news to those who are wandering aimlessly lost, that they might be found before it's too late.

Father, thank You for coming to me when I was lost, and letting me find the "pearl of great price" which is the love, the forgiveness, and the peace and joy I have found in You. Amen

Wash and Wear Religion

"I am overwhelmed with joy in the LORD my God! For he has dressed me with the clothing of salvation and draped me in a robe of righteousness. I am like a bridegroom in his wedding suit or a bride with her jewels." Isaiah 61:10 NLT

What joy there is in knowing that, because of our faith in Jesus Christ and His death on the cross for our sins, we have been cleansed and clothed in the righteousness of Christ. This means that when we stand before God, He will not see our sins, but will look at us just as He looks at His Son, in whom He was well pleased! *"let us go right into the presence of God, with true hearts fully trusting him. For our evil consciences have been sprinkled with Christ's blood to make us clean, and our bodies have been washed with pure water"* (Hebrews 10:22)

> *"Wash me thoroughly from my iniquity, And cleanse me from my sin."*
> *Psalm 51:2*

Who in the world would want to show up at a wedding with a dirty robe that has not been cleansed by blood of Jesus? Just as sin has no more dominion over our spirit, by the grace of God and by the power of His Spirit, we should not let it have dominion over our flesh

Thank God He has given us a "wash and wear" robe. Knowing that some of the road dirt of the flesh, the world and the devil is bound to soil our robe, He provides the "living water", which not only takes away our thirst but will keep our robes "white as snow" by daily washing through confession and repentance.

> *"Friend, how did you come in here without a wedding garment?' And he was speechless. Then the king said to the servants, 'Bind him hand and foot, ⁰take him away, and cast him into outer darkness; there will be weeping and gnashing of teeth."*
> *Matthew 22:12b,13*

May God forbid any of us from failing to get dressed for the wedding feast!

Father, thank You for cleansing me with the blood of Jesus, and for keeping me clean by the power of Your Spirit. Amen.

Are You the Missing Link?

"So if you break the smallest commandment and teach others to do the same, you will be the least in the Kingdom of Heaven" Matthew 5:19 NLT

While evolutionists are continually searching for the missing link, thousands are themselves becoming the real "missing links" by failing to obey God's command to teach their children the commandments of God.

> **"He commanded our ancestors to teach them to their children, so the next generation might know them—even the children not yet born—that they in turn might teach their children." Psalm 78:5,6 NLT**

One of the most satanic lies ever foisted is that we should not try to influence our children in religious matters, but let them find their own way. This is like thinking we should turn our children loose in a dung heap and they will somehow come out smelling like a rose!

When we break our covenant relationship with God by not passing our faith along to our children, we set in motion a downward spiral with consequences on not only our children, but upon generations to come.

Oftentimes, what we teach by example is worse than what we don't teach because of disobedience.

The consequences of missing links are all around us. The very institution of family itself is being threatened as never before. Let the restoration begin by every believer resolving as Joshua did: *"But as for me and my house, we will serve the LORD."(Joshua 24:15b)*

> *"Teach them to your children. Talk about them when you are at home and when you are away on a journey, when you are lying down and when you are getting up again"*
> *Deut 11:9 NLT*

Father forgive me for not bringing my children up in the nurture and admonition of You as well as I could have or should have. From this day forward, by the power of Your Spirit, help me to do better. Amen

God Wants to Give You The Desires of Your Heart!

"And I will give you a new heart with new and right desires, and will put a new spirit in you. I will take out your stony heart of sin and give you a new, obedient heart." Ezekial 36:26

> "Delight yourself also in the LORD, and He shall give you the desires of your heart."
> Psalm 37:4

One of the key principles of debt counseling is the necessity to know the difference between needs and wants. Bankruptcy courts are full of people who failed to make this distinction. Millions of others are in bondage to credit card and other debts that are suffocating and threatening to overwhelm them.

Many believers know by heart and believe: *"And my God shall supply all your need according to His riches in glory by Christ Jesus" (Philippians 4:19),* but miss out on the exceeding joy of understanding that God actually delights in giving us the desires of our new heart.

When we receive Jesus Christ as our Lord and Savior, we receive a heart transplant by the power of the Holy Spirit . This new heart is pure, clean, and debt free, and we no longer have to worry about our sin debt that was suffocating and threatening to overwhelm us. Our debt has been paid in full!

This new heart we receive is the one Ezekial was talking about...one filled with new and right desires. The love of God gives us no choice but

to respond in love and obedience and to want to do the things that please Him and give us the joy, the peace, the love of others, and the security that is the true desire of our new hearts.

> "Beloved, if our heart does not condemn us, we have confidence toward God. And whatever we ask we receive from Him, because we keep His commandments and do those things that are pleasing in His sight."
> 1 John3:20

Only unbelief, disobedience, and self centeredness can thwart God's delight in giving us the desires of our heart!

Father, by the power of Your Spirit, help me to understand that You not only want to supply my needs, but that You delight in granting the desires of my new heart when I am abiding in You. Amen

The Highway of Life

"And this is the way to have eternal life—to know You, the only true God, and Jesus Christ, the one You sent to earth." John 17:3 NLT

There is a "high" way of life and a "low" way of life. The "low" way of foolishness, self centeredness, stubbornness,and disobedience, leads to destruction.*" There is a way that seems right to a man, But its end is the way of death. (Proverbs 16:25)*

> *"As for God, His way is perfect. All the LORD'S promises prove true. He is a shield for all who look to Him for protection."*
> *2 Sam 22:31*

The "high" way is the only way to travel if we want to live forever. It begins the minute we receive Jesus Christ as our Savior and continues as we get to know God through getting to know Jesus Christ through His Word.

The "high" way is the road less traveled. As Jesus said: *"Enter by the narrow gate; for wide is the gate and broad is the way that leads to destruction, and there are many who go in by it.   Because narrow is the gate and difficult is the way which leads to life, and there are few who find it." (Matthew 7:12)*

Sometimes the "High" way of life can be very hard to travel. We often have detours of dalliance and doubt, and continually have to dodge the potholes of pride, selfishness, anger, lust, unforgiveness, and idolatry.

> *"Jesus said to him, "I am the way, the truth, and the life. No one comes to the Father except through Me."*
> *John 14:6*

Thank God that as he provided a cloud by day and a pillar of fire by night to guide the Israelites, He provides us with the Holy Spirit to guide us and to give us power to overcome the onslaughts of the world, the flesh, and the devil that would get us off course.

Father, guide me through the potholes of life that I might stay anchored deep in You and following Your "high" way. Amen

Wanna Dance?

"Praise his name with dancing, accompanied by tambourine and harp. For the LORD delights in his people; He crowns the humble with salvation." Psalm 149:3 NLT

Like it or not, we all are going to dance to the tune of someone. It may be with the siren of fleshly pleasure which will consume us if it can. We might be dancing to the beat of fame and fortune, or boogieing to win the approval of our peers. Lady Luck may be beckoning, or the ever popular money grabbers' stomp may be the tune.

> *"Observe and obey all these words which I command you, that it may go well with you and your children after you forever, when you do what is good and right in the sight of the LORD your God."*
> *Deuteronomy 12:28*

The older we get, the more we are going to realize that this dance in the ball room of life is going to end. The things we held so dear and thought so important are going to turn out to be wood, hay, and stubble from God's perspective.

It is time to remember the one who brought us to the dance, who said: *"You have seen what I did to the Egyptians, and how I bore you on eagles' wings and brought you to Myself. Now therefore, if you will indeed obey My voice and keep My covenant, then you shall be a special treasure to Me above all people; for all the earth is Mine"* (Exodus 19:5)

Outside of eternal life can you imagine any greater blessing than that which comes from obedience? Wouldn't you really rather be a "special treasure" to God and enjoy all the promises and privileges of sonship?

His arms are outstretched and bidding you to come dance and enjoy the joy of the Lord and the blessings of obedience in this life and the next.When you dance with God, you don't even have to worry about paying the fiddler.

> *"Or do you despise the riches of His goodness, forbearance, and longsuffering, not knowing that the goodness of God leads you to repentance?"*
> *Romans 2:4*

Father, I am not a very good dancer, but I know that You are a good leader. By the power of Your Spirit teach me to dance to Your tune all the days of my life. Amen.

Going to the Dogs

"But you, Timothy, belong to God; so run from all these evil things, and follow what is right and good. Pursue a godly life, along with faith, love, perseverance, and gentleness 1 Timothy 6:11 NLT

> *"Let us pursue the knowledge of the LORD. His going forth is established as the morning; He will come to us like the rain."*
> **Hosea 6:3**

Greyhound racing is a big business in Florida and a few other states. Millions of dollars are spent each year betting on which dog will get closest to the mechanical bunny at the finish line.

Night after night for several years, the greyhounds will run like the wind in a futile pursuit of catching that bunny.

Before we consider how dumb those dogs must be, lets clean out our closets of all the vain and fruitless "bunnies" we may be or might have been pursuing. How many times have we spent a big part of our time, talents, and treasures pursuing worldly fame and fortune, love in all the wrong places, or some other trivial pursuit?

God tells us that we are to pursue the kingdom of God and His righteousness so that all of the love, peace, and joy that He wants for us may be ours. He has promised to be a *"rewarder of those who seek Him"*, to *"grant us the desires of our heart"*,and to *"work all things to the good for those who love Him and are called according to His purposes."*

> *"See that no one renders evil for evil to anyone, but always pursue what is good both for yourselves and for all."*
> **1 Thessalonians 5:15 NLT**

If God is all powerful, and He is, if God cannot lie, and He can't; isn't He really the one we should be chasing? We don't have to run very far or very fast. Unlike those elusive bunnies He is standing at the door knocking and bidding us to come.

Father, in Your mercy, help me to give up my trivial pursuits and help me to focus on pursuing the peace and joy that can only be found in You. Amen

Get it Right the First Time!
"Don't be ornery like a horse or mule that needs bit and bridle to stay on track." God-defiers are always in trouble; GOD-affirmers find themselves loved every time they turn around." Psalm 32:9 MSG

Whether training horses, dogs, or children, manufacturing a car or other product, the importance of doing it right the first time cannot be overlooked. It is twice as hard and takes twice as long. We not only have to train but untrain. Look at the billions of dollars spent on automobile, tire and other product recalls.

> *"Train me, GOD, to walk straight; then I'll follow Your true path. Put me together, one heart and mind; then, undivided, I'll worship in joyful fear."*
> *Psalm 86:11(MSG)*

This may be why God's Word places so much emphasis on training children. *"Train up a child in the way he should go, And when he is old he will not depart from it." (Proverbs 22:6)*

What a blessing it is to be one of those who were planted in the "good soil" where we were fed and nourished early in life and have enjoyed the blessings of abiding all the days of our lives. If you are one of these, don't feel cheated that you don't have a dramatic testimony concerning your "before" and "after" life. Just praise God for His faithfulness in keeping His promises to believers and their children.

If you were one of those "ornery" ones like the prodigal son before receiving salvation, be thankful that God tracked you down and did whatever it took to bring you into that saving relationship with Him.

We should all try to spare our children the anguish of wandering aimlessly lost by encouraging them in God's Word and setting a good example of the joy and blessings of Christian living so that they might "get it right" from the "getgo"!

> *"With these weapons we break down every proud argument that keeps people from knowing God. With these weapons we conquer their rebellious ideas, and we teach them to obey Christ."*
> *2 Corinthians 10:5 NLT*

Father, now that You have claimed me as Your very own, by the power of Your Spirit, help me to "get it right" so that I can avoid the painful consequences of sin. Amen

Read Colossians 1   Psalm 145

Are You "Keeping the Faith"

"You are the light of the world—like a city on a mountain, glowing in the night for all to see. Don't hide your light under a basket! Instead, put it on a stand and let it shine for all." Matthew 5:14-15 NLT

There is a lot to be said for the "perseverance of the saints" who, by the power of the Holy Spirit, keep their faith throughout all of the disappointments failures and problems of life. We all need to "anchor deep"in the faith of a God who cannot lie, and a Savior who cannot fail.

> *"Everyone will share the story of Your wonderful goodness;*
> *they will sing with joy of Your righteousness."*
> *Psalm 145:7 NLT*

Unfortunately, there are too many Christians who are "keeping the faith" in the wrong way. They are "keeping the faith" to themselves and for themselves.

We have close knit communities of believers who believe that the church exists to uphold the traditions and doctrines of their denomination and to minister to them and their families without regard for the Great Commission.

We have believing individuals who are "closet Christians" who may bring their Christianity out on Sundays, but for the most part, keep their faith as a deep dark secret.

Faith is not something that we hoard, but something that we are commanded to share! Where would you be today if someone had not shared the "good news" with you?

And how do we share our faith? By being "sermons in shoes" through living a life that reflects our love for God and for others. We are told: *"Instead, you must worship Christ as Lord of your life. And if you are asked about your Christian hope, always be ready to explain it." (1 Peter 3:15 NLT)*

May God give us all the more passion to "pass on our faith" to others than we have to share our interests in our favorite ball clubs, hobbies, cars, children, and other topics of conversation. May we never bury our wonderful gift of salvation in the ground and suffer the fate of the unfaithful steward!

> *"Always thanking the Father, who has enabled you to share the inheritance that belongs to God's holy people, who live in the light."*
> *Colossians 1:12 NLT*

Father, help me to let my light shine in the power of Your Spirit. Amen

58

Do You Have A Record?

"He canceled the record that contained the charges against us. He took it and destroyed it by nailing it to Christ's cross." Colossians 2:14 NLT

Hopefully, you don't have a criminal record, but you do have a record

> *"LORD, if you kept a record of our sins, who, O Lord, could ever survive?*
> *Psalm 130:3 NLT*

of everything else. We have traffic violation records, school records, social security records, credit records, dental records, medical records, and "track" records on how we have done in the race of life.

What about our sin record? When we consider that every thought, word, and deed against the clear commandments and nature of God is sin, do we dare try to count the sins on record against us?

For most of us to make it through the day with less than 5 unkind thoughts, words, or deeds of jealousy, envy, lust, anger, selfishness, pride, etc., would be a very fine day. We are told that *"if we say we have no sin, we deceive ourselves and the truth is not in us" (1 John 1:8)* So if we sin just 4 times a day that's 1460 sins per year, and by age 50 that's 73,000 sins!

Would you really like to take a chance standing before God with this kind of record, without the righteousness of Christ? As believers that Jesus Christ died on the cross for our sins so that we would not have to die in the "lake of fire", we should live out our lives giving praise and glory to God in thanksgiving for what He has done for us.

We should wear the white robe of righteousness that He has covered us with and let our record be full of the good works for which God created us to do even before we were born. Our good works are the only works that we are going to be held accountable for at the resurrection of the just.

> *"And anyone whose name was not found recorded in the Book of Life was thrown into the lake of fire."*
> *Revelation 20:15 NLT*

Lord, thank You for your amazing grace that cleanses me from all sin and makes me righteous in Your sight by the blood of Your lamb. Amen.

Have You Ever Been Convicted?

"There is therefore now no condemnation to those who are in Christ Jesus, who do not walk according to the flesh, but according to the Spirit. For the law of the Spirit of life in Christ Jesus has made me free from the law of sin and death." Romans 8:1,2

If you were ever arrested for being a Christian, would there be enough evidence to convict you? This often asked, but still valid question can be very convicting in itself. Too often, too many of us would have to answer no. Although we "talk the talk", we "walk the walk" of the unbeliever, and no witness could be found to the fruits of the Spirit, good works for which we were created,

> *"Oh, do not hold us guilty for our former sins! Let Your tenderhearted mercies quickly meet our needs, for we are brought low to the dust"*
> *Psalm 79:8 NLT*

or fruits of righteousness that should be evidenced in the lives of all who claim the name of Christian.

The word convicted carries a double meaning, both good and bad. When it means to be found guilty (except for being a Christian) is bad; when used to mean to be convinced, it is good.

In His love, God has given us His Holy Spirit to convict us of our sinfulness which leads to saving faith in Jesus Christ, and to continually convict us of our specific sins that need daily cleansing and repentance.

The Holy Spirit also convicts us that we are unconditionally loved, forever forgiven, and totally accepted with the righteousness of Christ, when we receive Him as our Savior. He convinces us through faith that His grace is sufficient for all our needs, that He works all things for our good, that nothing will be able to separate us from His love, and many other promises that we can cling to and appropriate by faith.

> *"Yet now God in His gracious kindness declares us not guilty. He has done this through Christ Jesus, who has freed us by taking away our sins"*
> *Romans 3:24 NLT*

Oh what joy there is when we become convicted by the power of the Holy Spirit!

Father, thank you for making me a convict for Christ and saving me from the condemnation and damnation that I deserve. Amen

True Worship

"Now if you will fear and worship the LORD and listen to His voice, and if you do not rebel against the LORD'S commands, and if you and your king follow the LORD your God, then all will be well. " 1 Samuel 12:14 NLT

We are all worshippers! Whether it be the one true God or NFL Football, everyone has things that they give their adoration and devotion. If time, talents, and treasures are the measures of our worship, and if we are honest with ourselves, our worship of God leaves much to be desired.

> *"Happy are those who hear the joyful call to worship, for they will walk in the light of Your presence, LORD."*
> *Psalm 89:15 NLT*

We are all, at one time or another, children of a lesser god. We often put family, pleasure, fame and fortune, careers, ahead of the One who created us in His image, loves us with an everlasting love, and asks only that we worship no other gods, love Him, and love others.

It really comes down to a matter of control. Does your love of God control you and everything that you do, or do you spend more of your time and resources on other pursuits?

How would you compare your time spent in corporate worship with your time spent on recreational pursuits. How would you compare your time spent in home bible study, prayer, and devotions with time spent watching TV? How about the time spent talking about some race or ball game compared to the time sharing the love of God with others?

> *"These people honor Me with their lips, but their hearts are far away. Their worship is a farce ,for they replace God's commands with their own man-made teachings"*
> *Mark 7:7 NLT*

When it comes to money, who's in control?

Father, I am sorry to confess that I do not give You the first fruits of my time, talents, and treasures that I should. By the power of Your Spirit, help me to be a true worshipper of you in every area of my life. Amen

God's B & B

"So we, *being* many, are one body in Christ, and individually members of one another." Romans 12:5

Bed and Breakfast lodgings are increasing in popularity and usage throughout the world. Staying at one can be a wonderful experience if it is a good one.

> *"Sing to the LORD a new song. Sing His praises in the assembly of the faithful."*
> *Psalm 149:1b NLT*

God's B and B's are also meant to be a wonderful experience. We are talking about "Believing" and "Belonging"!. There seem to be a lot of people who don't connect the two, but God surely does.What is so hard to understand about *"And let us consider one another in order to stir up love and good works, not forsaking the assembling of ourselves together, as is the manner of some, but exhorting one another, and so much the more as you see the Day approaching."* (Hebrews 10:24,25)

Christ established His church and gave it the keys to the kingdom of God. which is the "Good News" of the gospel that we received and through which we became joint heirs with Christ. It as the chosen bride of Christ through which we receive encouragement, love, and accountability, and celebrate the presence of God in a very special way.

Christ's Church is where we share the joy of corporate worship, the opportunities for ministry and service, for growing in the Word, and for being on mission for the Great Commission.

Our call to salvation is a call to membership into the priesthood of believers and communion of saints. Belonging is not an option, it is a command, and we dare not ignore it and miss out on the blessings that obedience to this command brings.

> *"Let the word of Christ dwell in you richly in all wisdom, teaching and admonishing one another in psalms and hymns and spiritual songs, singing with grace in your hearts to the Lord."*
> *Colossian 3:16*

The Lone Ranger may have been a great childhood hero, but he has no standing in the family of God.

Father, thank you for providing Your church, where I can worship, grow, and be nurtured by the love and encouragement of other believers. Amen

Swiss Cheese Religion

"Have you not seen a futile vision, and have you not spoken false divination? You say, 'The LORD says,' but I have not spoken." Ezekial 13:7

Swiss cheese makes a wonderful sandwich, especially when combined with ham, bread and all the "fixings". But it is holey, not holy. The difference between "holey" and "holy" seems to escape millions of well meaning but seriously misinformed misinterpreters of the Bible, whose "Swiss Cheese" religions have so many holes there's hardly any real holiness.

> *"Through Your precepts I get understanding; therefore I hate every false way."*
> *Psalm 119:104*

We have those who blame all failed healings on the sick one's lack of faith. There is the "Santa Claus" contingent that teach God wants us all to be wealthy financially. There was the widespread teaching of a few years ago that Rock N. Roll records were satanic because if you played them backwards you would get a satanic message.(As if anyone would really play records backwards)!

At one time or another, life Insurance, dancing, boy scouts, Proctor and Gamble's trademark,and automobiles, have been called creations of the devil.

The really big holes that can have serious consequences are the teachings that Jesus Christ"s death on the cross was not sufficient for our salvation and that we have to do something to earn it; that somehow our salvation is all about what we do instead of what Jesus did; that it's all about feelings, or that it's all about our relationship with a denomination instead of our relationship with a Savior.

We need our 'Swiss Cheese" covered top and bottom with the real "Bread of Life" so that we can be "anchored deep" in the saving faith of knowing Jesus Christ as our Savior and Lord and that our "hope is build on nothing less than Jesus Blood and righteousness!"

> *"In this the love of God was manifested toward us, that God has sent His only begotten Son into the world, that we might live through Him"*
> *1 John 4:9*

Father, help me to stay anchored deep in Your truth. Protect me from the distractions of the world, the flesh, and the evil one that take me away from Your truth. Amen

What's Your Blood Type?
"Much more then, having now been justified by His blood, we shall be saved from wrath through Him."Romans 5:9

Just as air, food, and water are the outside essentials of physical life,

> *"Come now, and let us reason together," says the LORD, "Though your sins are like scarlet, they shall be as white as snow;"*
> *Isaiah 1: 18*

so blood is probably the key interior ingredient of sustaining life. Whether we lose it by injury or internal bleeding,a blood transfusion is all that can keep us alive. We all have one of four types of blood, and it is essential that any transfusion that we receive be of the same type.

There are over 350 biblical references to blood and it is significant in several ways.

First of all, we are all "blood relatives" of Adam and it has been through the blood of generation after generation that our corrupt sin nature has lived on in everyone. Secondly, the blood of circumcision signified the purifying of the child by the shedding of blood.(Hebrew 9:22)

The Passover blood of a sacrificial lamb posted on the lintels of their home, caused the angel of death to "pass over" the houses of the Israelites when God struck down the first born of all the Egyptians.

Abraham's faith in being willing to sacrifice his son was accepted as righteousness by God, and God promised that *"In your seed all the nations of the earth shall be blessed."* This promise was fulfilled in Jesus Christ, by whose blood sacrifice, all who would receive Him as Savior by faith would be accepted as righteous in the eyes of God.

> *"So Christ was offered once to bear the sins of many. To those who eagerly wait for Him He will appear a second time, apart from sin, for salvation."*
> *Hebews 9:28*

Whether your blood type is A, B, AB, or D. only a faith transfusion of the blood of Christ can purify your heart and free you from the inherited corruption of your sin nature and bondage to sin.

Father, keep me ever mindful that You made the supreme blood sacrifice on the cross by dying for my sins, so that I can live forever with You. Amen.

Read 1 Corinthians 13:1-13   Psalm 37:27-31
Who Says "Quitters Never Win"?

"The Lord isn't really being slow about his promise to return, as some people think. No, he is being patient for your sake. He does not want anyone to perish, so he is giving more time for everyone to repent." 2 Peter 3:9 NLT

It's all about context! While perseverance and endurance are admiral character traits for everyone, when they become

> "Depart from evil,
> and do good;
> and dwell
> forevermore."
> Psalm 37.27

pride driven, hard headedness, and stubbornness , they can easily turn anyone into a loser in the game of life now and forever. We should certainly never quit loving God and loving and forgiving others, or believing in Jesus Christ as our Savior.

Our call to faith is a call to repentance or a call to "quitting" our old ways and taking on a new life in Christ. People who quit smoking, quit gossiping, quit being so selfish and self centered, or who quit any of the hundreds of attitudes and activities that are not pleasing to God become winners by quitting.

In cards and stocks, knowing when to quit is a virtue. In relationships, knowing when to quit arguing, quit complaining, and quit demanding our way paves the way for a better relationship. Sometimes, we need to give up on people that are pulling us down, instead of building us up.

> "Even if I give away all
> that I have and
> surrender my body so
> that I may boast but
> have no love, I get
> nothing out of it."
> 1 Corinthians 13:3
> NIV

We need to quit sinning or die to sin daily so that we can know the great faithfulness of God, whose compassion never fails, and whose grace and mercy are renewed every day. He is the only one who never quits!

Father, give me the wisdom and spiritual discernment to know how and when to quit. Amen.

65

God Does Remember Some Things

"For God is not unfair. He will not forget how hard you have worked for Him and how you have shown your love to Him by caring for other Christians, as you still do." Hebrews 6:10 (NLT)

God's selective memory works just the opposite of ours. We tend to dwell on the bad things people do, and forget the good, while God, who "remembers our sins no more" remembers about everything else.

> *"He does not forget the cry of the humble."*
> *Psalm 9:12*

God remembers our names that He has written in the Book of Life. If He remembers every sparrow (Luke 12:6), He certainly will remember you!

He will not forget to help the children of Israel (Isaiah 44:21); He will not forget any promise He has ever made. *"For the LORD your God is merciful—he will not abandon you or destroy you or forget the solemn covenant he made with your ancestors."(Deuteronomy 4:31 NLT)*

We need to understand that God is always watching us and that He is greatly pleased when we do the things that reflect His character and His will for how we should live our lives. Whether it's visiting the sick or those in prison, feeding the hungry, helping the needy, or forgiving as we have been forgiven, we can be sure that He is not only pleased, but that He will remember.

When *"the resurrection of the just" (Luke 14:14)* takes place and we must give account for the stewardship of our lives, how comforting it is to know that our random acts of kindness, obedience, generosity, and love will be remembered! This is what "storing up treasures in heaven" is all about.

> *"Can a woman forget her nursing child, And not have compassion on the son of her womb? Surely they may forget, Yet I will not forget you."*
> *Isaiah 49:15*

Father, thank you for forgiving and forgetting my sins while not forgetting any good works that I have done that glorify You. Amen.

Read 2 Corinthians 3:4-18

The Great Remodeler

"He lifted me out of the pit of despair, out of the mud and the mire. He set my feet on solid ground and steadied me as I walked along." Psalm 40:2 NLT

Whether houses or people, remodeling is never easy. More and more you see perfectly good buildings being torn down to make way for new ones because it costs more to remodel than to build from scratch.

> *"Is this not the fast that I have chosen: to loose the bonds of wickedness, to undo the heavy burdens, to let the oppressed go free, and that you break every yoke?"*
> *Isaiah 58:6*

It's interesting to note that the greatest success in curing addiction and reforming criminals has been with faith based programs that recognize the sovereignty and power of the Great Remodeler!

While it is true that God does not make any junk, it is also true that every one is born with a sinful nature that only a heart transplant can cure. How fortunate are those who can receive this transplant before sin and darkened understanding take complete control and lead to more serious problems.

. That Saul could be "remodeled" into the Apostle Paul is living proof that *"Therefore if the Son makes you free, you shall be free indeed.". (John 8:36)*

While we may have never been jailed for our sins, we have all been captive to them and need the "heart transplant" and transformation by the power of the Holy Spirit that remodels our conduct to conform to our new idenity in Christ. This "remodeling" begins the minute we receive Jesus Christ as our Savior, and will continue until we meet our "Great Remodeler face to face in heaven."

> *"But we all, with unveiled face, beholding as in a mirror the glory of the Lord, are being transformed into the same image from glory to glory, just as by the Spirit of the Lord."*
> *2 Corinthians 3:18*

"Father, thank you for loving me enough to have the long suffering and patience to continue remodeling me into the image of Your son. Amen

Got any Excess Baggage?

"Cease from anger, and forsake wrath; do not fret—*it* only *causes* harm." Psalm 37:8

It is amazing to see how much baggage some people take on trips.

> *"Let us lay aside every weight, and the sin which so easily ensnares us, and let us run with endurance the race that is set before us,"*
> *Hebrews 12:1b*

Whether by train, plane, or on cruises one has to wonder how anyone could possibly need to pack that much.

Unfortunately the excess physical, emotional, and spiritual baggage we choose to carry can threaten our well being and often the well being of those around us.

Excess weight can cause heart attacks, strokes, loss of self esteem, and many other problems.

The baggage of worry, fear, guilt, rejection, or remorse can cause even more problems. Our health, our peace, our joy, and our relationships with others are all put at risk when we carry these excesses.

How many marriages have failed because either the bride or groom or both have come with this excess baggage?

Satan is a master at discouraging us by letting this baggage fester in our hearts and rob us of the peace and joy that is promised every believer in Christ.

God sent His Son, Jesus Christ into the world not only to save us, but to bear these burdens so that we wouldn't have to. *Psalm 55:2* tells us: "*Cast your burden on the* LORD, *And He shall sustain you;*" Before we let baggage come to fill up our closets, let us always remember to dump our excess baggage at the foot of the cross.

> *"Which of you by worrying can add one cubit to his stature?"*
> *Matthew 6:27*

Father, let me always remember that fear, worry and despair are not the fruit of Your Spirit and give me the power of Your Spirit to live a life unencumbered with this kind of excess baggage. Amen

How's Your Portfolio?

"For riches certainly make themselves wings: They fly away like and eagle toward heaven." Proverbs 23:5

These words of wisdom offered by Solomon centuries ago sound as if

> **'By humility and the fear of the Lord are riches, honor and life,"**
> **Proverbs 22:4**

they might have been written yesterday by one of millions of investors who have seen their 401 plans, college bound funds, and personal investment portfolios take a hit and vanish into the clear blue skies.

In both the financial and the spiritual worlds, "think long term" is good advice. The "blue chips" of our spiritual portfolios are the investments we make in using our time, talent, treasure, and passion in things that will glorify God and bless others. God says: *"With me are riches and honor, enduring riches and righteousness".* *(Proverbs 8:18 NIV)* Scripture is full not only of admonitions, but of ways that we are to invest our treasures in heaven.

Just as the stock market has a daily list of winners and losers, Scripture gives us a list of winning and losing investments. Starting with obedience to the Great Commandment, Great Commission, and saving faith, we can add trust in God, humility, and doing good works to our "blue chip" list.

Our losers need to be dumped at the foot of the cross daily. A critical and unforgiving spirit, pride and arrogance, anger, envy, lust, and idolatry of any form have to got to go. The time, talents, and resources we invest in these pursuits may have some short term appeal, but over the long haul they are going to be worthless and disastrous. Have you inventoried your spiritual portfolio lately?

> **"Command those who are rich in this present age not to be haughty, nor to trust in uncertain riches but in the living God, who gives us richly all things to enjoy."**
> **1 Timothy 6:17**

Father, by the power of Your Spirit, help me to eliminate my losing investments from my spiritual portfolio. Amen.

Let Freedom Ring!

"Stand fast therefore in the liberty by which Christ has made us free, and do not be entangled again with a yoke of bondage." **Galatians 5:1**

The idea that we are born with an inherited birth defect called sin is not

> **"And you shall know the truth, and the truth shall make you free."**
> **John 8:32**

a very popular concept these days. Enlightened humanists and liberal politicians have ignored the reality of original sin to our peril. Liberals and humanists say that all crime stems from a bad environment, and that if we improve the environment we will eliminate crime and have utopia. The razed housing projects in many major cities belie that myth.

The disobedience of Adam and Eve caused all mankind to be kicked out of paradise and to be separated from God *("Therefore, just as through one man sin entered the world, and death through sin, and thus death spread to all men, because all sinned." (Romans 5:12)*

The "good news" is that by His death on the cross, Jesus Christ has ended the separation from God and freed all who believe from eternal death! *"But now having been set free from sin, and having become slaves of God, you have your fruit to holiness, and the end, everlasting life.(Romans 6:18).*

Think about it! For the very first time, we are free from bondage and domination by sin. We can actually, with the power of the Holy Spirit living within us live a life fully pleasing to God and bearing the fruit of the Spirit.

Although we may momentarily stumble and fall into sins of the flesh, we are no longer sinners, but saints No longer can we use the excuse "I'm only human" to justify our continual sinful behavior. We are no longer slaves to sin, but slaves of righteousness and our love of God leaves us no choice but to want to do the things that please Him., Shouldn't we start rejoicing and living in our freedom?

> **"But he who looks into the perfect law of liberty and continues in it, and is not a forgetful hearer but a doer of the work, this one will be blessed in what he does."**
> **James 1:25**

Father, thank You for setting me free from sin so that I can become a slave to Your righteousness. Amen

Panning For Gold

"And the Lord said, "Simon, Simon! Indeed, Satan has asked for you, that he may sift *you* as wheat. But I have prayed for you, that your faith should not fail; and when you have returned to *Me*, strengthen your brethren." Luke 22:31

In the daily battles of life, our faith is continually being sifted or tested.

> "But He knows the way that I take; when He has tested me, I shall come forth as gold"
> Job 23:10

We often fail miserably. It is through this sifting that the impurities of our lives are washed away, and we are cleansed to live lives fully pleasing to God.

In testimony after testimony in Scripture and in the personal witnessing of others, we find that God does indeed sift to where only our faith sustains us. The sifting of Peter is a perfect example of how God will sometimes allow us to go to the absolute pit of shame and despair, so that we can become "sermons in shoes" to the transforming and restoring grace of God

In His love, God is continually inspecting, correcting, and perfecting us into the image of Christ.

Life itself is, in a sense, an exercise in panning for gold. Our value system is continually changing as we find that all that glitters is not gold. The older we get, the more we realize that so much of the "stuff" that we prized so highly is only "stuff", offering no lasting pleasure or satisfaction.

Whether it is burned in the refiner's fire, or sifted in a sieve, the "wood, hay, and stubble of our lives" is going to disappear, and only the golden nuggets produced by a life of faith lived in bearing the fruits of the Spirit, and producing the good works for which we were created will have any value in the First National Bank of Heaven!

> "That the genuineness of your faith, being much more precious than gold that perishes, though it is tested by fire, may be found to praise, honor, and glory at the revelation of Jesus Christ,"
> 1 Peter 1:7b

Father, by the power of Your Spirit, help me to endure Your panning, and to find the real gold of living a life pleasing to You and fruitful in every good work. Amen

71

Your Credit Has Been Pre-Approved!

"Finally, there is laid up for me the crown of righteousness, which the Lord, the righteous Judge, will give to me on that Day, and not to me only but also to all who have loved His appearing". 2 Timothy 4:8

Our good credit would not last very long if we took advantage of all the pre-approved credit offers we receive on an ongoing basis. From credit cards to automobiles to home loans, there seems to be a concerted effort to get us into debt. Millions of Americans can give living witness to the pitfalls of easy credit.

> *"I will greatly rejoice in the LORD, my soul shall be joyful in my God; for He has clothed me with the garments of salvation, He has covered me with the robe of righteousness,"*
> *Isaiah 61:10*

There is one pre-approved credit that we can be very happy about and excited to have. It's that our faith in Jesus Christ has been credited to us for righteousness in God's bank account! No matter when we go home to be with the Lord, we can be sure that we are going to go clothed in the white robe of righteousness earned for us on the cross and that we will stand before God cleansed and in perfect holiness thanks to the blood of the Lamb.

Our line of credit was established over 2,000 years ago. There is no annual fee or interest charge. There are no credit turn downs, and there is overdraft insurance.

There is nothing we can do to earn this priceless gift of righteousness. Jesus Christ did it all! When He said: "it is finished" He meant that He had done all that God required to redeem us and reconcile us to God.

> *"just as David also describes the blessedness of the man to whom God imputes righteousness apart from works:"*
> *Romans 4:6*

Father, thank You for crediting my account with the righteousness of Your Son. so that I might have eternal life. Amen

Be A Pleasure Seeker!

"Do not fear, little flock, for it is your Father's good pleasure to give you the kingdom." Luke 12:32

What a difference perspective makes when it comes to pleasure. From

> *"Let them shout for joy and be glad, who favor my righteous cause; and let them say continually, Let the LORD be magnified, Who has pleasure in the prosperity of His servant."*
> *Psalm 35:27*

a self centered perspective, it most always has to do with the gratification of our flesh and what makes us happy.

From a Christ centered perspective, it has to do with seeking the pleasure of God. Jesus said: *"And He who sent Me is with Me. The Father has not left Me alone, for I always do those things that please Him."(John 8:29)*

And what are those things that please God? Loving God and others are certainly at the top of the list. Scripture tells us that "God tests the heart and has pleasure in righteousness." *(1 Chronicles 29:17)*, that *"He delights in exercising lovingkindness, judgment, and righteousness." (Jeremiah 9:24)*, and that *"He delights in the way of a good man." (Psalm 37:23)*

We are told in *Hebrews 13:16*: *"But do not forget to do good and to share, for with such sacrifices God is well pleased"* In *Psalm 149:4* we learn::*"For the LORD takes pleasure in His people; He will beautify the humble with salvation." Psalm 147:11* tells us that: *"The LORD takes pleasure in those who fear Him, In those who hope in His mercy."*

Just as Jesus knew the joy of hearing His Father say that He was well pleased with Him, we too can look forward to hearing our Father *say "well done thou good and faithful servant"* when we seek the pleasure of God by being obedient to His will and doing those things that give Him pleasure. Whose pleasure are you seeking?

> *"But without faith it is impossible to please Him, for he who comes to God must believe that He is, and that He is a rewarder of those who diligently seek Him."*
> *Hebrews 11:6*

Father, help me to seek the real pleasure that comes from living a life fully pleasing to You and fruitful in every good work. Amen.

Things God Hates

"These six *things* the LORD hates, yes, seven *are* an abomination to Him: a proud look, a lying tongue, hands that shed innocent blood, a heart that devises wicked plans, feet that are swift in running to evil, a false witness who speaks lies, and one who sows discord among brethren." Proverbs6:16-19

We know that God being the God of love, hates only one thing, and that is sin. He especially hates the sins against His commandment to love our neighbor,along with the sins against His commandment to love Him.

> "For whoever finds Me finds life, and obtains favor from the LORD; but he who sins against Me wrongs his own soul; all those who hate Me love death."
> Proverbs 8:35,36

The good news is that God hates sin but He loves sinners. *"As I live,"says the Lord GOD, 'I have no pleasure in the death of the wicked, but that the wicked turn from his way and live". (Ezekial 33:11)*

God is still standing at the door knocking calling sinners to repentance and salvation through faith in Jesus Christ. There is no sin that God is not longing to forgive.

He forgave Joseph's brothers. He forgave David, Abraham, Peter and the other Apostles, and the prodigal son. He stands ready, willing, able, and even longing to forgive all who call upon His name with Godly sorrow and true repentance.

God's well of forgiveness will never run dry. His love is wider than the ocean, and deeper than the sea. He says: *"All that the Father gives Me will come to Me, and the one who comes to Me I will by no means cast out." John 6:37*

*Kno*w that as much as God hates sin, He loves you even more. He loved you enough to have His own Son die on the cross so that you won't have to die. When we think of how much we have been forgiven, how can we help but love our forgiver even more?

> "Therefore, I say to you, her sins, which are many, are forgiven, for she loved much. But to whom little is forgiven, the same loves little."
> Luke 7:47

Father, thank you for your forever forgiveness and the power of Your Spirit with which I can win the battles over sin. Amen

Now You're "Meddlin"

"Watch and pray, lest you enter into temptation. The spirit indeed *is* willing, but the flesh *is* weak." Matthew 26:41

As a good friend once pointed out: "It's not temptation if you're not

> *"How many are my iniquities an sins? Make me know my transgression and my sin."*
> *Job 13:23*

tempted!" Think about it! The leprosy of sin that continues to spread throughout the world seems to infect different people with different weaknesses.

We can listen to sermons condemning weaknesses that we don't have and become infected with a big dose of hypocritical glory if we are not careful. We often have a hard time being sympathetic towards those who succumb to sins that don't tempt us.

It's hard for someone who has not become addicted to alcohol, tobacco, or drugs to understand how someone could be so weak or so dumb as to succumb to such things.

We have a tendency to be judgmental and critical of those who are grossly overweight, who allow themselves to be caught up in an illicit sexual relationship, or any other temptation with which we dont struggle. There is a little bit of the Pharisee in all of us that makes us feel just a little better than those infected with weaknesses we dont have.

When the subject turns to pride, envy, gossip, unforgiveness, or the many forms of idolatry that abound among us, we can get very defensive and start wishing that the preacher would "quit meddling", and sometimes even go into denial that we have a problem. The truth is that we all have sinned and fall short of the Glory of God. The Good News is that: we have forgiveness in Christ, and that He said: *"My grace is sufficient for you, for My strength is made perfect in weakness" (2 Corinthians 12:9)*

> *"But remember that the temptations that come into your life are no different from what others experience. And God is faithful. He will keep the temptation from becoming so strong that you can't stand up against it. When you are tempted, he will show you a way out so that you will not give in to it.*
> *1 Corinthians 10:13 NLT*

Father, lead me not into temptation, and deliver me from evil. Amen

God is Able!

"Daniel, servant of the living God, has your God, whom you serve continually, been able to deliver you from the lions?" Daniel 6:20b

Why, oh why do we doubt God's promises and His ability? Why is it so hard to accept that God, who created the world and everything in it, is not limited in any way? If He has His eyes upon the sparrow, is He not also able to keep His eyes on us.?

> *"Be exalted, O LORD, in Your own strength! We will sing and praise Your power."*
> *Psalm 21:13*

The ability of God to work His perfect will in our lives is not limited by His ability, but only by our unbelief. When Jesus asked: *"Do you believe that I am able to do this?"* (Matthew 9:28,) only belief was required for the healing to take place.

What confidence we can have when we believe when Paul says: *"So now, brethren, I commend you to God and to the word of His grace, which is able to build you up and give you an inheritance among all those who are sanctified." (Acts 20:32)*

What comfort there is in knowing: *"For in that He Himself has suffered, being tempted, He is able to aid those who are tempted."'* (Hebrews 2:18)

What hope there is in hearing: *"Now to Him who is able to do exceedingly abundantly above all that we ask or think, according to the power that works in us."* (Ephesians 3:20)

> *"And do not fear those who kill the body but cannot kill the soul. But rather fear Him who is able to destroy both soul and body in hell."*
> *Matthew 10:28*

What joy we can have in knowing *"Him who is able to keep you from stumbling, and to present you faultless before the presence of His glory with exceeding joy!"(Jude 1:24)*

Father, I believe that You are able to do all that You have promised. Thank you for the strength I receive in believing this. Amen

God Is Willing!

"Then Jesus, moved with compassion, stretched out *His* hand and touched him, and said to him, 'I am willing; be cleansed.'" Mark 1:41

We have a God who was willing to heal the sick, restore sight to the blind, and reward the faithfulness of all who came to Him in faith. If he was willing to sacrifice His own Son that we might live forever, how can anyone question His love, His grace, and His mercy?

> *"To them God willed to make known what are the riches of the glory of this mystery among the Gentiles: which is Christ in you, the hope of glory."*
> *Colossians 1:27*

How can we help but believe that He wills the very best for us, and is willing to do whatever it takes to accomplish His good will? About the only thing God is unwilling about is that any of us should perish. He wants us all to come to repentance.and enter into that love relationship with Him through faith in His Son.

The willingness of God is not the problem. The problem is in the unwillingness of man to receive the wonderful gift of salvation, and the unwillingness of all of us to let the yoke of submission to the will of God be placed upon us. *"The Spirit is indeed willing, but the flesh is weak"* (Mark 14:38)

We stumble and fall, we "waffle" and we make excuses, and our longsuffering and patient God continues to forgive and forget, and to lovingly chasten and discipline that we might be sanctified and conformed more into the image of Christ as he renews His grace and mercy to us each and every day.

> *"that it might be fulfilled which was spoken by Isaiah the prophet, saying:*
> *"He Himself took our infirmities And bore our sicknesses."*
> *Matthew 8:17b*

God's willingness to love us and to guide us along the paths of righteousness is exceeded only by His faithfulness in seeing that we do not perish, but have the everlasting life that is ours in Christ.

Father, through the power of Your Spirit living within, me help me to be as willing to receive as You are to give. Amen

God is Ready!

"Then the LORD said to me, "You have seen well, for I am ready to perform My word." Jeremiah 1:12

Our God is an awesome God! He is all powerful, all knowing, ever present, and never changing. He is ever loving, and thankfully ever ready! He is ever ready to forgive, and He is ever ready to save!

> *"For You, Lord, are good, and ready to forgive, and abundant in mercy to all those who call upon You".*
> *Psalm 86:5*

The great wedding feast has been prepared and the invitations go out on a daily basis. All of the privileges and blessings of the new covenant of grace are awaiting those who come to the wedding. We have the forgiveness of our sins, the favor of God, the peace that surpasses all understanding.

We have access to the throne of grace, and the comfort of the Spirit. The preparations have been made for a heaven on earth now, and for heaven in the future. To reject this invitation into a personal love relationship with God through faith in Jesus Christ is the worst thing anyone can do other than to come to the wedding clothed in hypocrisy instead of the white robe of righteousness.

God is not only ready to forgive, He is ready to comfort, to protect, to supply all our needs, and to work all things for our good. He is ready to make us conduits of His love to others.

How about you? Have you "rsvp'd" your invitation? Are you now enjoying all of the joys and privileges of a right relationship with God through faith in Jesus Christ, or are you one of those who is not quite "ready" to go to the wedding? There is limited seating, so you best get ready while there are still seats available.

> *"See, I have prepared my dinner; my oxen and fatted cattle are killed, and all things are ready. Come to the wedding."*
> *Matthew 22:4b*

Father, thank you for including me on your guest list and giving me the power of Your Spirit so that I can accept the invitation. Amen

Do You Have God in Your Religion?

"But He will say, 'I tell you I do not know you, where you are from. Depart from Me, all you workers of iniquity." Luke 13:27

Someone once said that "whoever makes religion his god will not have

> *"I will praise You, O LORD, with my whole heart;"*
> *Psalm 9:1*

God in his religion". I believe this statement to be true. Sometimes we see people so engrossed in the traditions and doctrines in their church that they squeeze God, His love and the Great Commission right out of the picture.

We have "Don Quixotes" attacking the windmills of the mind, looking for error in every area in the beliefs in their own church and especially in the life and beliefs of other churches. The idea that God is not strong enough to defend the faith without their help is foreign to their thinking. Down through the centuries, we have had zealots dying by the thousands in the crusades, killing by the thousands as in the Spanish Inquisition, and burning so called heretics at the stake.

Somehow, the zealots get the idea that understandings contrary to their own, no matter how scripturally valid they might be, and having nothing to do with salvation and the centrality of the gospel, cannot be tolerated without compromising the truth of their own confessions and beliefs. So-called Christians quarrelling and fighting with each other in the name of religion makes the fury of a woman scorned seem like child's play.

Christianity is not a religiosity; it is a close personal relationship with Jesus Christ and the belief that He died for our sins. so that we would not have to. It's not the label we wear on our backs, it's all about who we have in our hearts.

> *"Do not speak evil of one another, brethren. He who speaks evil of a brother and judges his brother, speaks evil of the law and judges the law."*
> *James 4:11*

Father, never let my religiosity be a stumbling block to others. Let me give praise and honor and respect to all who confess Your Son as their hope of glory. Amen

Beware of the Leaven

"Then they understood that He did not tell *them* to beware of the leaven of bread, but of the doctrine of the Pharisees and Sadducees" Matthew 16:12

Yeast is an amazing ingredient. Just a tiny amount can hardly be recognized in a big batch of dough, but it affects all of the dough. When added, it goes to work silently and is hard to detect. It will gradually permeate the dough and take control of the whole loaf.

> *"A true witness delivers souls, but a deceitful witness speaks lies."*
> *Proverbs 14:25*

The false teachings and hypocrisy of the Scribes and Pharisees had exactly the same effect. Puffed up with pride, self-righteousness,and hypocrisy, they corrupted practically the whole body of believers against Christ and caused Him to be rejected, ridiculed. and crucified.

There is no room for this leaven in the body of Christ. We are to be sincere, humble, and without guile in the living and exercising of our faith. Unfortunately, both the leaven of false doctrine and hypocrisy are at work in the body of Christ at every level – personal, congregational, and denominational

On one hand we have those who place upholding tradition and doctrine way above the Great Commandment and Great Commission. On the other we have those with the mistaken notion that love means condoning what God calls sin and abominations.

Which of the two extremes is worse in the sight of God might best be left to the providence of God. Who can deal with either much better than us. *God* makes one thing very clear: *"For I say to you, that unless your righteousness exceeds the righteousness of the Scribes and Pharisees, you will by no means enter the kingdom of heaven." (Matthew 5:20)*

> *"Therefore let us keep the feast, not with old leaven, nor with the leaven of malice and wickedness, but with the unleavened bread of sincerity and truth."*
> *1 Corinthians 5:8*

Father, by the power of Your Spirit, give me the spiritual wisdom and discernment to recognize and resist the leaven of hypocrisy, self righteousness, and false doctrine. Amen

God is Faithful!\

"Because of the LORD's great love we are not consumed, for His compassions never fail. They are new every morning; great is Your faithfulness." Lamentations 3:22,23 NIV

There are living testimonies to the faithfulness of God all around us.

> "I will sing of the LORD's great love forever; with my mouth I will make Your faithfulness known through all generations."
> Psalm 89:1 NIV

There are not enough sheepfolds to hold all of the lost and wandering sheep who have strayed from the flock and been found and restored by the faithfulness of the Good Shepherd.

Scripture after Scripture speaks of the unfailing love and faithfulness of God. Because God is faithful, His promises are sure. *"The LORD is faithful to all His promises and loving toward all He has made." (Psalm 145:13)* What joy and comfort we have in knowing that God is faithful and that His promises are sure!

We can believe that He works all things for our good, that He loves us with an everlasting love, that He hears and a[ ] nothing can separate us from His love that i[ ] Christ.

> "Now it is God Who makes both us and you stand firm in Christ. He anointed us, set His seal of ownership on us, and put His Spirit in our hearts as a deposit, guarranteeing what is to come."
> 2 Corinthians 1:21,22 NIV

Because of God's faithfulness and [ ] expectations for the future that He has prepar[ ] live the abundant life here on earth, se[ ] condemnation that Christ bought for us on the[ ]

"Since we have these promises, dear fri[ ] from everything that contaminates body and [ ] of reverence for God." (2 Corinthians 7:1 NIV)

Father, help m to give You thanks for Your faithfulness by living life to the fullest in and for You. Amen

81

Diplomatic Immunity

"*There is* therefore now no condemnation to those who are in Christ Jesus,who do not walk according to the flesh, but according to the Spirit." Romans 8:1

Diplomatic immunity is in effect throughout most of the world. It gives

> "*In the* LORD *all the descendants of Israel shall be justified, and shall glory.*"
> Isaiah 45:25

special status to foreign diplomatic agents giving them the highest degree of privileges and immunities, including personal inviolability; which means that they may not be arrested or detained, or their work and lives hindered in any way.

As believers in and ambassadors of Jesus Christ, we also enjoy the highest degrees of privileges and immunities. We become members of a royal priesthood and joint heirs with Christ.

When satan tries to undermine our faith by continually reminding us of our failures and shortcomings as a means of making us doubt our faith and salvation, we need to repent and invoke our "diplomatic immunity"

We need always to remember that when we confess our sins they are forgiven and erased from God's memory bank, and only satan, never God, will bring them up again as though they were not forgiven.

We need to remember that when we received Jesus Christ as our Savior we were given the Holy Spirit *"in whom also, having believed, you were sealed with the Holy Spirit of promise, who is the guarantee of our inheritance until the redemption of the purchased possession, to the praise of His glory."(Ephesians 1:13b,14)*

In other words, if we are <u>true</u> believers, we have been set free from condemnation and the power of sin to destroy us, and free to bear the fruits of righteousness and produce the good works for which we were created. With the power of the Holy Spirt and Christ in us, we have the immunity we need to live the abundant life that is ours in Christ.

> "*Who shall bring a charge against God's elect? It is God who justifies. Who is he who condemns?*"
> Romans 8:33

Father, thank you for covering me with the blood of Your Son that I am immunized from eternal damnation. Amen.

Read 1 Corinthians 2:4-16   Psalm 119:116-120

Meeting Expectations

"Now to Him who is able to do exceedingly abundantly above all that we ask or think, according to the power that works in us, to Him *be* glory in the church by Christ Jesus to all generations, forever and ever. Amen." Ephesians 3:20

We sometimes feel overcome by the expectations others place on us.

> "Uphold me according to Your
> word, that I may live;
> and do not let me be
> ashamed of my hope."
> Psalm 119:116

Our parents, our peers, our spouses, our bosses, our customers or parishioners have expectations we can't possibly meet.

How great it is when some person or product exceeds our expectations. "Better than expected" is music to the ears to the research companies that are continually monitoring customer satisfaction on behalf of automobile, manufacturers,cruise lines, banks, etc.

What about our expectations of God? Do we have Him confused with Santa Claus? Do we think we will have no more problems once we become a child of God? Do we get angry with God when He allows bad things to happen to us or loved ones?

The better we get to know God through His Son, who came to reveal Him to us, the more realistic and more fulfilling our expectations of God will become. When we learn the secret of abiding, we will find that God's plans, promises ,disciplining and pruning, and His on going presence within us are all part of His "working all things for the good of those who love Him and are called according too His purposes" for now and forever.

He came fulfill the law that we couldn't keep for ourselves. He died on the cross and was raised to life on the third day by God the father to validate that our sin debt was paid in full.

> "Eye has not seen,nor
> ear heard, Nor have
> entered into the heart
> of man the things
> which God has
> prepared for those who
> love Him."
> 1 Corinthians 2:9b

That He has ascended into heaven to prepare a place for us in an eternity with no more pain,no more tears, no more sickness, and no more sin should really excite us about our Great Expectations!

Father, thank you for Your love, grace, and mercy, which exceed all my expectations. Amen

83

I Know Someone Who Does

"Surely it was for my benefit that I suffered such anguish. In your love you kept me from the pit of destruction; you have put all my sins behind your back." Isaiah 38:17 NIV

Some times, we find ourselves trying to comfort someone who has experienced such tragedy or pain that we

> *"He is despised and rejected by men, a Man of sorrows and acquainted with grief."*
> *Isaiah 53:3*

can't begin to know how they feel, because, by the grace of God, we have never yet had to go through such a thing.

Whether it's the death of a spouse, or a child, a devastating illness or accident, or the rejection of a spouse, we can imagine but never really know how they feel. Sometimes, just the comfort of our presence and our silence is the best comfort. During these times, we need to remember that we know someone who does know how bad it hurts.

Jesus knew the physical pain of beating, scourging, and being nailed to a cross. He knew the emotional pain of abandonment by his friends and rejection by the world. He knew the humiliation of being paraded through the streets of Jerusalem stark naked. He was betrayed, lied about, made to suffer for the sins of the world, none of which He ever committed. He was finally crucified at the town dump.

Sometimes God puts us through some of these ordeals in order that we might be a comforter and encourager for someone else going through the same thing. Because we have "been there and done that", people will listen and take heart from what we say.

All the time, we have, through faith in Jesus Christ, a Savior who can empathize with our pain or sorrow and give us the comfort of the Holy Spirit Living within us and fill our hearts with peace. This is part of the really good news we believers can appropriate by faith for every situation.

> *"For we do not have a High Priest who cannot sympathize with our weaknesses, but was in all points tempted as we are, yet without sin"*
> *Hebrews 4:14*

Father, thank you for the comfort of Your love and the strength of Your Spirit in my times of pain and suffering. Amen

Grace Abuse

"What shall we say then? Shall we continue in sin that grace may abound? Certainly not! How shall we who died to sin live any longer in it." Romans 6:1,2

The grace of God has not only brought us salvation, but it has bought

> *"Remember me, O LORD, with the favor You have toward Your people."*
> *Psalm 106:4*

us freedom! For the first time, we have the power within us to live in freedom from not only the penalty of sin, but from the power of sin.

When we experience the new birth through faith in Jesus Christ, we die to sin and become alive in Christ. Although sin still abounds in this world and in our flesh, the grace of God much more abounds in our spirit and we are free to live in the freedom of our new life in Christ.

Although our God is long suffering and patient, how can we think that our profession of faith we made years ago is all we need when there is absolutely no corroborating evidence in the way we live our lives? James tells us: *"But be doers of the word, and not hearers only, deceiving yourselves. For if anyone is a hearer of the word and not a doer, he is like a man observing his natural face in a mirror; for he observes himself, goes away, and immediately forgets what kind of man he was. But he who looks into the perfect law of liberty and continues in it, and is not a forgetful hearer but a doer of the work, this one will be blessed in what he does." (James 1:21-25)*

We sometimes, in our freedom, allow our flesh to take control and cause us to fall into sin momentarily. We deal with this by confession and repentance and by going on. But we should never abuse the grace of God by willfully choosing to sin as though we had a license. The excuse that "I am just a sinner and can't help it" will no longer cut it. In Christ, we are saints who have been set free from bondage to sin. The sooner we start living like we believe this, the more abundant our lives will become.

> *"And having been set free from sin, you became slaves of righteousness."*
> *Romans 6:18*

Father, keep me ever mindful that Your grace is not cheap, that it cost you the life of Your own dear Son. Let me never abuse it. Amen

The Gold Standard

"How much better to get wisdom than gold! And to get understanding is to be chosen rather than silver." Proverbs 16:16

Prior to 1971, the United States of America was on the Gold Standard, and our paper money was backed by and redeemable for gold. Today, our paper money is backed by nothing more than the credit of the United States government and has continued to become worth less and less as government debt has increased more and more.

> *"The idols of the nations are silver and gold. The work of of men's hands."*
> *Psalm 135:15*

Up until around 1950, God's Word was the standard for morality and civil and criminal law in this country. Today, our standard for morality and civil and criminal law in this country has seemingly forgotten God and been replaced by the wisdom of man with disastrous results.

Our new age of enlightenment has given us abortion on demand, respectable homosexuality, a 66% divorce rate, relative truth, AIDS, drug addiction and substance abuse, pornography addiction, etc. We have seen the Word of God banned and condoms distributed in our public schools. Out of wedlock births have skyrocketed. Our "liberation" from God's moral restraints have brought more bondage and misery instead.

Through it all, those who persevere in the faith have the ultimate gold standard, backed by the death of and validated by the resurrection of Jesus Christ. Whether the streets of heaven are paved with gold doesn't matter. What counts is that we have a future and a hope that is incorruptible and will never fail.

> *"That the genuineness of your faith, being much more precious than gold that perishes, though it is tested by fire, may be found to praise, honor, and glory at the revelation of Jesus Christ,"*
> *1 Peter 1:7*

Father, let my sadness and concern over the abandonment of Your standards by so much of this world be comforted by the assurance I have through faith that You are still in Control. Amen

Happy Are Those Who are Persecuted?
**"Blessed *are* those who are persecuted for righteousness' sake,
For theirs is the kingdom of heaven." Matthew 5:10**

In spite of our efforts and attempts to live at peace with all men. we are going to be persecuted for righteousness sake. Although we do nothing to seek persecution, and should never provoke it by our conduct or by unnecessarily offensive speech to others, we are going to experience it in some way or another.

> *"My times are in Your hand; deliver me from the hand of my enemies, and from those who persecute me."*
> *Psalm 31:15*

The world is at enmity with God, and does not take kindly to the truth that it really doesn't want to hear. When our behavior is Christ-like, and we are living in friendship with God, we should consider it a blessing to be counted worthy to suffer for the cause of Christ.

Whether it's exclusion from some social circles, being mocked or ridiculed to your face or behind your back, or being killed or tortured as many martyrs throughout the centuries have been and continue to be today, persecution of Christians is growing.

One of the saddest, and most widespread persecutions seem to be going on within Christ's church. How our Lord must grieve to see and hear those who claim the name of Christian strike out against fellow believers in order to advance their own self centered ambitions. Worst of all, some of the biggest offenders feel that they are defending the faith or traditions and commit their persecutions in the name of God, just like the Scribes and Pharisees of the Bible.

And why in the world should we be happy when we are persecuted? Our Lord Himself gives the answer in *Matthew 5:11:* "*Rejoice and be exceedingly glad, for great is your reward in heaven,*"

> *"My brethren, count it all joy when you fall into various trials,"*
> *James 1:2*

Father, when persecution comes, give me the strength and power to endure and rejoice. Amen

Happy Are the Pure in Heart
"Blessed *are* the pure in heart, for they shall see God." Matthew 5:8

> *"Or who may stand in His holy place? He who has clean hands and a pure heart."*
> *Psalm 24:3b,4*

The Scribes and Pharisees were long on show and tell, but their hearts were corrupt. They were pleasers of themselves and others, instead of pleasers of God. How could they or anyone think that God, who knows everything, does not know the condition of our hearts?

We can rationalize and deny, fool everyone, even ourselves; but, we can't fool God. He knows when our hearts are far from Him. He knows when we put other things ahead of Him. He knows when we are "talking the talk", but not "walking the walk."

Purity of heart can only be gained and maintained by the daily cleansing of our hearts that comes through godly sorrow and true repentance for our sins.

The Good News is that God has sent His Holy Spirit to mend our broken hearts, cleanse our dirty hearts, and do a major heart transplant where necessary. As He chips away at our rough edges, He does what only He can do – change our hearts.

By His grace, he can turn our anger into self control, our pride into humility, our self centeredness into Christ centeredness, and our hate into love. He can change our deceitful and wicked hearts into pure hearts, and then, we will begin to see and experience His love all around us in this life and meet Him face to face in the next.

> *"Finally, brethren, whatever things are true, whatever things are noble, whatever things are just, whatever things are pure, whatever things are lovely, whatever things are of good report, if there is any virtue and if there is anything praiseworthy—meditate on these things."*
> *Philippians 4:8*

Father, create in me a pure heart, and renew a right spirit in me daily. Amen.

Happy Are Those Who Hunger and Thirst

"Blessed *are* those who hunger and thirst for righteousness, for they shall be filled." Matthew 5:6

We have been given an appetite for food and water so that our bodies might be sustained and nourished. Without food and water, we perish.

> *"O God, You are my God;*
> *early will I seek You;*
> *my soul thirsts for You;*
> *my flesh longs for You"*
> *Psalm 63:1*

When we experience a new birth in Christ, we are given an appetite for the true Bread of Life and living water for our souls. To hunger and thirst for more and more of Christ is the work of sanctification (or making us more holy and Christ-like) that the Holy Spirit works in us.

Our hunger and thirst for righteousness fills us with the joy of our salvation, when we receive Jesus Christ as our Savior. Once we have received salvation, the Holy Spirit who has come to live within us fills us with the hunger and thirst to be more like Christ and to lead a life pleasing to God. We need the sustenance of the Word and the power of the Holy Spirit to accomplish this.

In the flesh, we hunger and thirst after many other things, which we think important and necessary. We hunger for material treasures, for the applause of others, for anything that we think will fill us with happiness. The trouble is, that when we seek happiness and fulfillment in these things at the expense of seeking the righteousness of Christ, we are going to be disappointed.

> *"Whoever drinks of this water will thirst again, but whoever drinks of the water that I shall give him will never thirst. But the water that I shall give him will become in him a fountain of water springing up into everlasting life."*
> *John 4:13*

Love is the only thing that never fails. When we are filled with the Love of God in Christ Jesus we are truly filled.

Father, by the power of Your Spirit, instill the fervent desire to know You through the Son that You have sent, so that I may be continually filled. Amen

Happy Are The Poor in Spirit?
"Blessed *are* the poor in spirit, for theirs is the kingdom of heaven." Matthew 5:3

When we come to the realization that we are sinners who need a Savior, we receive the kingdom of heaven, under the New Covenant of grace.

> *"You shame the counsel of the poor, But the LORD is his refuge."*
> *Psalm 14:6*

As long as we continue to live in our own self centered world and validate ourselves without acknowledging that we have a sin problem, the joys of the kingdom of heaven in this world and the next will elude us.

We are told *"But seek first the kingdom of God and His righteousness, and all these things shall be added to you." (Matthew 6:33)* Unfortunately, many of us treasure other people and things, first, and never enter into the fullness of joy that comes only from putting God first in every area of our lives.

God is looking for a broken spirit and a contrite heart. As we learn from His comments about the Scribes and Pharisees, being puffed up with pride, and thinking more highly of ourselves than we ought, is not the way to approach God.

When we approach God in true repentance and with godly sorrow for our sins, we will by no means be cast out, and we receive the keys to the kingdom and all its benefits. We receive "God's riches at Christ's expense," and always realize that it is the "Gift of God, lest any man should boast."

> *"Do not lay up for yourselves treasures on earth, where moth and rust destroy and where thieves break in and steal."*
> *Matthew 6:19*

Father, the poverty of my separation from You has turned into enjoying the blessings of a right relationship with You through faith in Jesus Christ. Keep me ever mindful and thankful of Your amazing grace. Amen.

90

Read 2 Corinthians 1:3-7   Psalm 77:1-15

Happy Are Those Who Mourn

**"Weeping may endure for a night, but joy *comes* in the morning."
Psalm 30:5**

The blessings of mourning are something we have to think about. We

> *"I cried out to God with my voice and He gave ear to me."*
> *Psalm 77:1*

grieve the loss of a friend or loved one and are comforted by the blessed assurance that they have gone on to a better life with no more sorrow, no more tears, and no more pain. For this, we should not only be comforted, but mourn with thanksgiving and praise to God.

The mourning over the loss of a friend or loved one, who has not died in the Lord, is another matter. We are filled with a tremendous sense of loss and sometimes with the feeling that we could have and should have done more to share our faith and try to shepherd them into a saving relationship with God, through faith in Jesus Christ, and now it's too late. We can only take comfort in knowing that God judges the heart and that there had hopefully been a change of heart we didn't know about.

The most probable meaning of Jesus' words ,here, are the comfort we receive when we mourn over our sins. To have a broken spirit and contrite heart over our repeated failures to measure up to God's standards of conduct and obedience is a good thing. God forbid that we let sins go unconfessed and unrepented and the hardness of heart sets in so that we no longer mourn for our sins.

God takes our godly sorrow over our sins and comforts us with His love. When we are honest with God, as we have to be since He knows our hearts, He is able to work that true repentance in our hearts and give us the peace that only the forgiveness of God can afford.   When your comfort zone gets squeezed by your sins, think about the blessings of this promise that those who mourn will be comforted by the Holy Spirit living within you.

> *"Who comforts us in all our tribulation"*
> *2 Corinthians 1:4*

Father, give me godly sorrow to mourn over my sins. By the power of Your Holy Spirit, comfort me and work true repentance in my heart. Amen

91

Happy Are the Meek

"Take My yoke upon you and learn from Me, for I am gentle and lowly in heart, and you will find rest for your souls." Matthew 11:29

There are a lot of misconceptions about what "meek" means. To

> *"But the meek shall inherit the earth, and shall delight themselves in the abundance of peace"*
> *Psalm 37:11*

many, it means being "wimpy" and letting people walk all over you. To others, it means being humble and having a gentle spirit. Perhaps, the understanding to be "meek" means not to be conceited or stuck on oneself is the best understanding of all.

Our Lord was the perfect example of meekness. As He said: *"I am gentle and lowly in heart."* When we in meekness submit to the yoke of Christ and to His loving discipline, we become teachable, preachable, and usable. As surely as God will resist the proud, He will pour out His grace on the meek. (1 Peter 5:5, James 4:6)

The pride and self righteousness of the Scribes and Pharisees were quite a contrast to the meekness and gentleness of Christ. As followers of Christ, we should strive to enjoy the blessedness of the meek, and to love others as Christ loves us.

> *"And a servant of the Lord must not quarrel but be gentle to all, able to teach, patient, in humility correcting those who are in opposition,"*
> *2 Timothy 2:24,25a*

There is a marked difference in the health, well being, and quality of life of the meek, who are calm, cool, and collected, when compared with the proud, self centered types who lead more turbulent, stress filled lives.

Father, help me to claim the promise of my inheritance for blessings in this life by appropriating the meekness of Christ in my life, by the power of Your Sprit. Amen.

Blessed Are the Peacemakers

"Salt *is* good, but if the salt loses its flavor, how will you season it? Have salt in yourselves and have peace with one another." Mark 9:50

Sometimes, it seems that there is no peace. Conflicts between countries, within families, within churches, on the job, and within the hearts of men abound all around us.

> "Depart from evil and do good; seek peace and pursue it."
> Psalm 34:14

We can be sure that all of the hatred and strife, all of the arrogance and pride, and all of man's inhumanity to man are not from God. They are the manifestations of the evil One, who is still working overtime throughout the world and in the hearts of both believers and unbelievers.

President Jimmy Carter will be best remembered by me as a godly man who made peace between Egypt and Israel. To me, he is a walking testimony to the truth of Proverbs 16:7: *"When a man's ways please the* LORD, *He makes even his enemies to be at peace with him."* Of all the qualities of a peacemaker, being a godly man who pleases the Lord ranks at the top of the list. Just as *"a soft answer turns away wrath" (Proverbs 15:1),* so does the "humble approach" seem to be indispensable in resolving conflicts and making peace.

The saddest commentary of all is the terrible witness and offense given by professing Christians participating in intra church strife. The words and deeds that come out of many pastors and leaders, as well as lay people, is an affront to God, which severely hinders the building up of His Kingdom, and brings rejoicing only to satan.

The good news is that we have, in Jesus Christ, the ultimate peacemaker. *"For He Himself is our peace, who has made both one, and has broken down the middle wall of separation."(Ephesians 2:14)* No wonder He said that peacemakers would be called the sons of God!

> "For God is not the author of confusion, but of peace, as in all the churches of the saints."
> 1 Corinthians 14:33

Father, let the peace that I have in You carry over to being a peacemaker in every arena of my life. Amen.

The Quality of Mercy

"Return to the LORD your God, for He *is* gracious and merciful, slow to anger, and of great kindness; and He relents from doing harm." Joel 2:13

Although most consider grace and mercy to mean the same, to me, it is helpful to make the distinction that grace means getting undeserved favor, and mercy means not getting deserved punishment or consequences.

> *"Let, I pray, Your merciful kindness be for my comfort, according to Your word to Your servant."*
> *Psalm 119:76*

Our Lord said: *"Blessed are the merciful, for they shall obtain mercy."(Matthew 5:7)* In other words, the best way of being sure to receive mercy is to be merciful. Our Lord showed mercy to the thief on the cross. The spouse who forgives a cheating mate is showing great mercy. The parable of the unjust steward speaks clearly about the importance of being merciful and the consequences of being unmerciful.

When I think of all the whippings I deserved and didn't get because my mother showed mercy, of the many sinful and unkind things I have done and said, but did not get the consequences I deserved, I am grateful for God's mercy.

When I consider that after almost 75 years of sins and sinning, I still must plea, "Lord have mercy upon me," I am so thankful that God, in His grace, move, and mercy, has removed my sins as far as the east is from the west. He remembers them no more, and His love, grace, and mercy is from everlasting to everlasting.

We receive the undeserved favor of God by faith in Jesus Christ and by believing that He died on the Cross for our sins. Salvation is a free gift that we did nothing to earn or deserve, and we have only to receive by faith. How can we possibly be unforgiving and unmerciful to anyone,

> *"For He is kind to the unthankful and evil. Therefore be merciful, just as your Father also is merciful."*
> *Luke 6:35b,36*

when we consider what we have received, rather than what we deserved?

Father, keep me ever mindful to be merciful so that I might receive the mercy I need. Amen.

The Supreme Six Pack

"It is good to give thanks to the LORD, and to sing praises to Your name, O Most High." Psalm 92:1

You won't find this six pack in the cooler at your favorite convenience

> *"Oh, that men would give thanks to the LORD for His goodness, and for His wonderful works to the children of men!"*
> *Psalm 107:8*

store, and although it's non-alcoholic in content, it's almost 100% proof in producing a spiritual high. If you go through a six pack a day of this, you will soon become a much happier, more cheerful person.

Whether you pray in the morning, in the evening, or on the run, take the time to offer a six pack of praise to God for six blessings, large or small, that you have received and enjoy, and try to come up with six different ones every day. Start with all the needs God supplies on a daily basis.

No matter how bad things may seem, or how badly you may feel, there are still blessings abounding, if you think about it. How many people has God given to love you or given you to love?...Thank Him for one or two a day! How many abilities and talents has God given you?...Thank Him for one a day! (If you can read or write, walk and see, cook or sew, sing or dance, you have abilities and talents to be thankful for.)

How many answers to prayers have you received?...thank Him for one a day, even when He has answered "no". How many ways does God love you?...Thank Him for one a day! How many other ways has God blessed you?...Thank Him for one a day! Once you start really thinking about all of

the blessings God has showered upon you, including the wonders of nature, the miracle inventions that we take for granted, etc., at six a day, you might never get around to thanking Him for all of them.

> *"Rejoice always, pray without ceasing, in everything give thanks; for this is the will of God in Christ Jesus for you."*
> *1 Thessalonians 5:16*

Father, thank You for my overflowing cup of blessings. Let me never take them for granted, but be truly thankful. Amen

A Few of God's Favorite Things

"For God so loved the world that He gave His only begotten Son, that whoever believes in Him should not perish but have everlasting life." John 3:16

Eternal life consists of getting to know God through His Son whom He has sent. It begins the moment we receive Jesus Christ as our Savior and will continue forever. Our response to God's gift of salvation should be to love Him and to please Him by loving the things He loves.

> *"I love those who love me, and those who seek me diligently will find me."*
> *Proverbs 8:17*

God loves Jesus: *"For the Father Himself loves you, because you have loved Me."* (John 16 27)

God loves obedience: *"Jesus answered and said to him, 'If anyone loves Me, he will keep My word, and My Father will love him, and We will come to him and make our home with him.'"* (John 14:23) *"The steps of a good man are ordered by the LORD, and He delights in his way."* (Psalm 37:3). *"He loves righteousness and justice."* (Psalm 34.4)

God loves to give good gifts to His children. *"If you then, being evil, know how to give good gifts to your children, how much more will your Father who is in heaven give good things to those who ask Him!"* (Matthew 7:11)

"God loves a cheerful giver." (2 Corinthians 9:7)

Although He hates sin, God loves sinners: *"But God, who is rich in mercy, because of His great love with which He loved us, even when we were dead in trespasses, made us alive together with Christ (by grace you have been saved), and raised us up together, and made us sit together in the heavenly places in Christ Jesus."* (Ephesians 2:4)

> *"Therefore do not be unwise, but understand what the will of the Lord is."*
> *Ephesians 5:17*

How about you? Are these some of your favorite things? Is there any reason they shouldn't be?

Father, help me to love the things You love, and to despise that which is evil and to grow in Your Word constantly so that I might know these things. Amen.

Follow the Directions!

"All Scripture *is* given by inspiration of God, and *is* profitable for doctrine, for reproof, for correction, for instruction in righteousness, that the man of God may be complete, thoroughly equipped for every good work." 2 Timothy 3:16

In this "assemble it yourself" age, there seems to be a new occupation

> *"To receive the instruction of wisdom, justice, judgment, and equity,"*
> *Proverbs 1:3*

for people with a sadistic streak. It's designing and writing assembly or operating instructions! Sometimes, the type is so small you can't read it. Other times, they do not make sense. Often, we just wing it and end up with too many extra nuts and bolts, and usually, have to undo everything and start from scratch.

God has given us "assembly instructions" for the abundant life. His directions are very clear, but sometimes hard to follow because they often seem to get in the way of what we perceive to be the abundant life. Often, we try putting a happy life together without following the instructions and suffer a lifetime of painful consequences.

God first gave specific instructions to Adam and Eve, and their failure that followed them set off a chain reaction of consequences for which, we are still suffering. God then gave specific instructions to the children of Israel, and their failure to follow them kept them wandering around in the wilderness for forty years.

Finally, in His mercy, God came to earth in the flesh of His own Son to not only die to save us, but to live to show us how we should live and to give us written instructions on how to live.

> *"Then they asked Him, saying, "Teacher, we know that You say and teach rightly, and You do not show personal favoritism, but teach the way of God in truth."*
> *Luke 20:21*

Starting with the instructions to love God, and to love others, Jesus wrote the perfect instruction manual. It's called the "Holy Bible!"

Father, help me to better learn your instructions by spending more time in Your instruction book. Amen

Under New Management

"And you *He made alive*, who were dead in trespasses and sins, in which you once walked." Ephesians 2:1,2a

When we become dead to sin and alive in Christ through receiving Jesus Christ as our Savior, we experience a new spiritual birth and receive a new spiritual birth right by the power of the Holy Spirit. This birth right is the indwelling presence of the Holy Spirit, who comes to take over the management of our lives.

> *"O LORD, You brought my soul up from the grave; You have kept me alive, that I should not go down to the pit."*
> *Psalm 30:4*

Under the management of the Holy Spirit, sin has no more dominion over us. We are free to be all that we can be in Christ and empowered to do what God has called us to do in producing the good works for which we were created. We are instantly restored and renewed, and we are continually being restored and renewed as God continues to conform us to the likeness of His Son.

We find ourselves giving up more and more control of the flesh and submitting more and more to the management of the Spirit, who is constantly at work guiding us into all truth, convicting us of our sins, and making intercession for us with God the Father.

The transformation worked by the Spirit within the hearts of believers is why they call grace "amazing." We find that the things we wanted to do become things we no longer care about doing, as we discover the better, more satisfying, way of living in Christ. We find ourselves exercising our freedom to reject the influence of Satan and our flesh more and more and to opt for living in the peace and joy of the Lord, bearing the fruit of His Spirit.

> *"Likewise you also, reckon yourselves to be dead indeed to sin, but alive to God in Christ Jesus our Lord."*
> *Romans 6:11*

Can those around us see that we are under new management?

Father, thank you for the gift of the Holy Spirit, and for making me a temple for His presence. Amen.

Class Reunion

"Not that I speak in regard to need, for I have learned in whatever state I am, to be content." Philippians 4:11

Bill was the most likely to succeed in the class of 1953, and he came to the reunion to show that he did it! Even if you didn't ask, he would remind you of his success and many "toys". Tom also attended the reunion. He was living on Social Security in a modest mobile home park.

> *"There is one who makes himself rich, yet has nothing; and one who makes himself poor, yet has great riches."*
> *Proverbs 13:7*

There is no question of who had been the most successful from the world's viewpoint. The question is who has been the most successful from God's viewpoint. Who did the "toys" own, and who owned the real treasures?

How much is enough for you? Is "just a little bit more" your response to what it would take to make you happy? Are you going through life thinking, "I would be happy if I only had _____(a nicer car, a bigger house, a better job, a better spouse, etc., etc.)

It is only when we base our happiness on whom we are in Christ that we will ever have the real wealth of peace and godly contentment, and real security.

To know that in Christ we are unconditionally loved, totally accepted, and forever forgiven; and to know that we are significant because of the relationship we have with God the Father through faith in God the Son, is to have more than enough. In knowing this, we are truly rich.

> *"Now godliness with contentment is great gain."*
> *1 Timothy 6:6*

Father, give the the security and contentment of Your love so that I won't have to depend on the things of this world for my happiness and validation. Amen

Fair Weather Friends

"God will surely do this for you, for He always does just what He says, and He is the one who invited you into this wonderful friendship with His Son, Jesus Christs our Lord." 1 Corinthians 1:9 NLT

It's amazing how friends seem to vanish when you can't be anymore

> "As iron sharpens iron, a friend sharpens a friend."
> Proverbs 27:17

use to them. The prodigal son had plenty of friends to play with on his way to the pig pen. Politicians out of office and purchasing agents out of jobs often find out about fair weather friends.

Jesus has had and continues to have more "fair weather" friends than anyone in the history of mankind. When He provided free lunch, five thousand became His new "best friends", and would probably later be among those shouting, "Crucify Him". The disciples were no where to be found when trouble came.

It seems that many today base their friendship with Jesus on what He can do for them instead of what He has done for them. As long as the "free lunches" and the cup of material and physical blessings keep overflowing, "God is in His heaven and all's right with the world."

When troubles and probems arise, as they surely will and do, many respond with anger and falling away from God instead of anchoring deeper and deeper into their love relationship with Him and experiencing the strength and comfort of His promises.

Every rose garden has thorns. Until God takes us home to heavenly bliss, He promises His all sufficient grace to handle the scratches.

> "And here is how to measure it-the greatest love is shown when people lay down their lives for their friends."
> John 15:13 NLT

When we learn the secret of abiding in God through getting to know Him through His Son, we will find out what real friendship is all about.

Father, let me be more than a "fair weather friend". By the power of Your Spirit, let me be a friend in all seasons for all the right reasons. Amen

"God Never Wastes a Hurt"

"The suffering you sent was good for me, for it taught me to pay attention to your principles." Psalm 119:71 NLT

The "life to the fullest" that we have in Christ begins the minute we receive Him as our Savior and never ends. We receive a lot of great things in addition to eternal life.

> *"You have allowed me to suffer much hardship, but you will restore me to life again and lift me up from the depths of the earth."*
> *Psalm 71:20 NLT*

We have the presence of the Holy Spirit – Christ in us to pray for us, comfort and correct us, call all things to our remembrance, and to fill us with strength and power from on high.

We have the promise that God will work all things for our good, that He will do whatever it takes to mold us into the image of Christ. God promises to meet our every need, to provide a means of escape from temptation, to keep us in the security of His love and His forgiveness until we see him face to face.

The one thing that God does not promise is to keep us from knowing pain, suffering and sorrow in this life. That promise is reserved for heaven.In doing whatever it takes to bring us to saving faith, and then to keep us there and growing into the fullness of Christ, God often allows problems that inspect, correct, protect, and make us more like Christ.

How can we be like Christ if we went through life knowing no pain or suffering or temptation? How better can we be a comforter and blessing to others than having gone through the pain and suffering they are presently experiencing?

How could we help becoming proud and self centered without the humbling discipline of God which keeps us Christ centered and aware of our total dependency upon Him. To what good use has God put your pain and sufferings?

> *"So when we are weighed down with troubles, it is for your benefit and salvation!"*
> *2 Corinthians 1:5 NLT*

I am indebted to Rick Warren, author of "The Purpose Driven Life" for the thought that "God never wastes a hurt."

Father, thank you for doing whatever it takes to conform me to the image of Christ, and to equip me to produce the fruits for which you created me. Amen

Friends in High Places

"God will surely do this for you, for he always does just what he says, and he is the one who invited you into this wonderful friendship with his Son, Jesus Christ our Lord."1 Corinthians 1:9 NLT

The politics of having friends in high places has gone on for a long time, and will continue regardless of all the campaign reform laws and other measures.

Special interest groups representing minorities and other bloc voters

> *"You didn't choose me. I chose you. I appointed you to go and produce fruit that will last, so that the Father will give you whatever you ask for, using my name."*
> *John 15:16 NLT*

seem to wield a very disproportionate influence because they elect people who cater to their interests..

Professional lobbying is a zillion dollar industry with millions in contributions spent to elect or gain access to friends in high places.

One of the great shames of our political system is the selling out of common interest to the special interest groups who control enough votes to intimidate and control certain agendas in this country.

As believers, it is very encouraging to know that we have two of the best friends in the very highest of places. They can't be bought, intimidated and they will never sell out to the opposition.

The Holy Spirit is continually making intercession for us even when we don't know for what to pray.

Best of all, Jesus Himself is our great high priest who is sitting at the right hand of God making intercession on our behalf so that God will not see us as the sinners we are, but as brothers and sisters of Christ.

> *"And the Father who knows all hearts knows what the Spirit is saying, for the Spirit pleads for us believers in harmony with God's own will."*
> *Romans 8:26 NLT*

His one time sacrifice of dying on the cross for us fulfilled all the righteous demands of the law and has restored our relationship with God.

Aren't you glad you've got such good friends in high places?

Father, what joy there is to knowing that my friendship with Your gives me access to your throne of grace. Amen

Are You a Door Knocker Downer?
"We use God's mighty weapons, not mere worldly weapons, to knock down the Devil's strongholds." 2 Corinthians 10:4 NLT

The disciples had a lot to learn about knocking down obstacles. Peter cut off the ear of one who was going to arrest Jesus. Luke 9:53 tells of James and John wanting to bring down fire from heaven and burn up a Samaritan village because they would not receive Jesus.

> *"Turn away from evil and do good. Work hard at living in peace with others."*
> *Psalm 34:10 NLT*

David had ample opportunities to end Saul's pursuit and persecution of him, but would not lay a hand on God's anointed one, but put to death the one that did. We are all greatly blessed by the Psalms David wrote while hiding out and fleeing the unjust persecution and attempts to kill him.

Before we respond to anything by over reacting or reacting to anything without our brains fully loaded, we can learn a lot from David about the rewards of long suffering and patience. He was "the man after God's own heart".

A lot of problems need to be left alone and given a chance to work themselves out. Premature rushes to judgment or over reaction often provide fuel for a fire that would otherwise soon burn out. A short fuse is dangerous in fireworks and in life.

God's "mighty weapons" of truth, righteousness, the Good News, faith, salvation, the Word of God, and prayer somehow don't seem all that powerful to our finite minds, but we live in a kingdom that has been built and is being built with them.

> *"A final word: Be strong with the Lord's mighty power. Put on all of God's armor so that you will be able to stand firm against all strategies and tricks of the Devil"*
> *Ephesians 6:10,11 NLT*

Oh that God would give us wisdom and spiritual discernment to know when to speak and when to remain silent, how to react without over reacting, and how to be proactive in fulfilling the Great Commission and tearing down the walls of hate and prejudice.

Father, keep me from from rash responses and actions. Amen

Watch Out for Side Effects!
"A prudent person foresees the danger ahead and takes precautions; the simpleton goes blindly on and suffers the consequences." Proverbs 22:3 NLT

I can't believe all the advertisements for new drugs and how they list the possible side effects of nausea, diarrhea, blurred vision, coughing, etc. It Sure doesn't make me want to rush out and buy.

> *"You will enjoy the fruit of your labor. How happy you will be! How rich your life!"*
> *Psalm 128.2 NLT*

People are still smoking worldwide in record numbers in spite of the conclusive evidence and warning that cigarettes cause a lot of health problems, including death.

It's a shame that all of the beer ads don't have to carry the same warning as drugs - that possible side effects include spouse and child abuse, car wrecks, loss of control of senses, etc.

The side effects of sexual immorality, which can include aids, herpes, unwanted pregnancy, broken homes and guilt should give anyone with a weakness in this area a warning to keep their guard up.

Even a new birth in Christ can trigger some hurtful side effects. We may lose some friends and undergo some severe testing as satan unleashes more of his darts at us. The Apostles learned all about these side effects.

Thank God that the good side effects of living in a right relationship with Him through faith in Jesus Christ far overcome any temporary pain, sadness, or discomfort!

> *"Don't be misled. Remember that you can't ignore God and get away with it. You will always reap what you sow!"*
> *Galatians 6:7 NLT*

We have peace that surpasses all understanding, the joy of the Lord, friendship with God, and the power of His Spirit living within us. We have the assurance that He will work all things for our good. We will know His unfailing love in this life and the life to come.

Father, protect me from sin and its consequences. Help me live in the freedom and joy of a right relationship with You through Your Son. Amen.